SAVAGES
APES
OR PEOPLE OF
Promise

A BIBLICAL STUDY OF BLACK ANCESTRY

SAVAGES APES
OR PEOPLE OF
Promise

A BIBLICAL STUDY OF BLACK ANCESTRY

JOCELYN D. WHITEHEAD

SOUTHFIELD, MICHIGAN

CITI OF
BOOKS

CITIOFBOOKS, INC.
3736 Eubank NE Suite A1
Albuquerque, NM 87111-3579
www.citiofbooks.com
Hotline: 1 (877) 389-2759
Fax: 1 (505) 930-7244

Ordering Information:
Quantity sales. Special discounts are available on quantity purchases by corporations, associations, and others. For details, contact the publisher at the address above.

Edited by: Dr. Monica Handy
Cover Design and Interior Layout by: LaTanya Orr, Selah Branding & Design LLC
Author Photo Credit: Honeycomb Images & Productions
Printed in the United States of America.

ISBN-13:   Softcover   979-8-89391-888-5
                eBook   979-8-89391-889-2

Library of Congress Control Number: 2025918028

DEDICATION

This book is dedicated to my mother,
Geraldine (Gerry) Marie Williams,
who finished her race on this earth
- February 8, 2020.

To my father, Ossian Williams who
taught me how to be still, how to think,
how to listen, how to figure things out,
how to stand on my own,
and to never quit!

ACKNOWLEDGMENTS

There is such a sense of accomplishment with the completion of my first published book. However, it would still be an unpublished manuscript without my loved one's help and support.

First and foremost, I thank the Holy Spirit for the anointing and for taking the pen and writing the words in this book. I truly understand how God's inspiration manifests in the Spirit and brings forth its work in due season.

I thank my ministry colleagues, friends, and those who learned of this project. Their prayers served as a covering that impacted and encouraged me on this journey. I am further humbled by their tiptoe expectation to read and experience the final published writing.

I give special thanks to my sister, Valda Atkinson, for not just the encouragement but for challenging me and believing in me, even when she may not have fully agreed or understood.

Thank you Crystal Grissom for your loving support from the very conception of this project.

Next, I must give a shout-out to my son, Mychal, who is my biggest cheerleader in all my endeavors. I love you more than words could ever express.

Thank you, Dr. Sabrina Evans, for being my "ram in the bush" in helping me get over the finish line.

Last, but not least, I would like to thank my friend and supporter Rev. Dr. Fredericka Jackson, who gave me unconditional support, encouragement, and countless conversations. She challenged me to stay the course and finish the race.

I am forever grateful to all of you and love you with my whole heart - mind, body, and soul.

Blessings and peace be upon you, both now and forevermore.

TABLE OF CONTENTS

INTRODUCTION

Several years ago, I began writing a book, of a different nature. I included a section relative to understanding the complexity of our African American culture. As I was writing, The Holy Spirit drew me in a different direction. I was led to look at who we (African Americans) are as a people in the Bible – which gave me a better understanding of our behaviors and the disconnectedness we have within our own community and the world. The motivating questions then became: Who are we and what is it that shapes our behaviors?

I recall distinctly being drawn to the prophetic books in the Bible of Jeremiah, Isaiah, and others. I stated in a matter-of-fact tone, *"Someone needs to break this stuff down."* It genuinely mirrors the African Americans' journey in life.

Without a doubt, I knew God was revealing a mystery to me, but there were so many deliberately hidden facts propagating misinformation about the African American population; it made the task grueling, frustrating, and seemed never-ending.

Some writings took time to comprehend, making it difficult to put the pieces together and find the missing parts. There were so many teasers. I felt as though I needed a Ph.D. in archeological data mining to grasp the information. Yet the Holy Spirit drove me to get to the bottom of it, and ironically, each discovery took me to the top of a mountain where I became awe-struck by the view. Then suddenly, it felt like I was dropped off a cliff and left dangling by a rope in midair.

Even in this challenging position, I needed to know what was above my head as well as beneath my feet. My Spirit constantly nudged me to dig deeper beneath the surface, where I ultimately discovered the missing pieces of truth. Then, I would climb back up this proverbial mountain to insert the missing parts.

In the process, I began to understand the difficulty in bridging the gap from the top of the mountain down to the valley, while asking the question, "Who are the so-called African American people? Why are we despised? What makes our genius so threatening, as well as our peculiarity?"

The fact that God was intentionally revealing information to me did not make it any less of a monumental task to decipher and assemble the details. I had a lot of fragmented information that was clearly part of a more truthful comprehensive picture. However, I did not begin to connect the dots until 2018, when I studied under Omar Thibodeaux, a pastor in New Orleans whom I deem a scholar and subject matter expert. He proved to be the answer to my prayer in terms of breaking down the mystery of who we are as a people. Through him, I began to understand our history from another level which continues to grow daily.

I rejoice in being able to share this truth which was always hidden in plain view! So, I proudly recite the tag line, call, and response Pastor Omar crafted—

"Who the People? We the People."

The people of promise. The people of God.
The people of the Covenant with Abraham, Isaac,
and Jacob. The original so-called Hebrews.

This information is not only mind-blowing, it is also liberating in the truest Biblical sense of the word. The identity of African Americans is finally being revealed and accepted by many in our community, but not enough.

This truth is evidenced in various writings and teachings and being increasingly revealed each day. God is moving, restoring sight to the blind, opening the ears of the deaf and the mouths of the mute.

My earnest prayer is that the information found in this book will fuel you, the reader, to change your mindset, behavior, and belief system and receive the Promises of Scripture God has for you.

The truth will set you free! Free from what you might ask? Free from oppression, free from the lies that have been repeated in the past 400 years. Lies that were under construction as early as the 1700s. In substance, that is a lot to uncover. But if you open your hearts and minds and receive the truth incarnate and the truth proclaimed, you will find this to be a very complex, yet simple truth.

I pray this writing does not leave you dangling but lifts the veil from your eyes to see the beauty of who we (African Americans) truly are as a people. I envision this journey extending into a community that will climb together, leaving no one behind.

I invite non-African Americans who are reading this book, to journey with us in learning the truth about the people called African Americans.

This book is intended to reveal the truth in a manner that will not intimidate or inundate the reader. I hope it will provoke the reader's desire to dig deeper into the subject matter and then climb up.

As you will discover, African Americans are not Savages or Apes but have a special place in this world.

A people without the knowledge of their past history, origin and culture, is like a tree without roots.

MARCUS GARVEY

CHAPTER ONE

HISTORICAL BACKGROUND
IN THE BEGINNING

T*he Beginning* is the first thing one must consider when examining a historical background, *"The Beginning" is what becomes our history in the long run.* When we look at the historical background of war, we search to find where or how it started. We gain knowledge of the parties involved and the actions and decisions that instigated a declaration of war.

We track the beginnings of relationships and, from time to time, look back on their history - sometimes marveling at the progression. That is because we can recall where the relationship is now versus where it started.

Historians record events to have a historical background based on facts. However, facts sometimes get altered, lost, or destroyed – intentionally or accidentally.

When we look back on the historical background of African Americans, our *recorded* history starts when slaves were first counted in the United States of America's census. The tally occurred in the late 1800s after the Civil War. Historical Records for African Americans post and pre-America arrival are missing. The void of information extends between the true beginning of our history in the Garden of Eden to the beginning of the recorded time, leaving thousands of years of historical data unaccounted for.

Therefore, when looking at the true beginning of where our heritage began, we only have a partial view. When we add 400 years of slavery in a foreign land that excluded our heritage, it results in a massive gap of critical missing data. This gap made it convenient and easier to force a new indoctrination into this new land. Beneath this new indoctrination level, a base level exists that holds the truth – the buried, bloodied, drowned, and hidden truth. To quote the mid-19th Century poet and journalist William Cullen Bryant, *"truth crushed to the earth will rise again."*

The truth is rising – not as William Cullen Bryant speaks of but rising from the annals of a Just God!

Consider the following sketch as a visual representation:

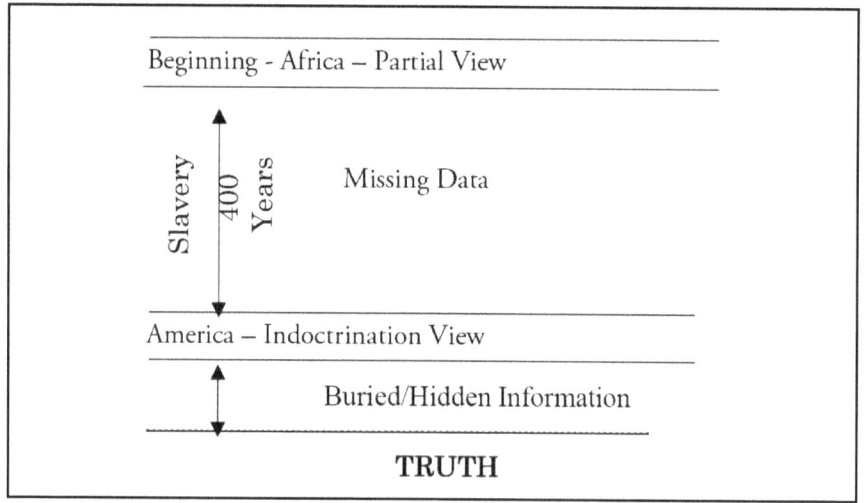

To bridge the gap in the illustration, we must first endeavor to gain a greater understanding of the information presented and, second, take a short journey back to the historical record of creation because African Americans are part of it.

Unfortunately, our history is missing the critical data pre-dating the census taken in the 1800s. That is absurd. The census only marks the beginning of over 400 years of slavery in a land called America, but it does not mark our ancestral beginning.

In the beginning ... God created the Heavens and the Earth (Genesis 1:1). As God continues in His remarkable creations, in Genesis 1:26-27, He describes His creation of man.

> *"So, God created mankind in his own image, in the image of God he created them; male and female he created them. God blessed them and said to them, "Be fruitful and increase in number; fill the earth and subdue it" (NIV).*

That is what God says in the Bible; man was created in the Image of God! Please notice, it does not say, "apart from some, who were descended from Apes," as some have suggested.

According to Genesis 2:8:

> *"... the LORD God planted a garden in Eden, in the East, and there He put the man whom he had formed" (ESV).*

Let's set some context by examining the possible location of the Garden of Eden. Genesis 2:10-14 states:

> *"A river flowed out of Eden to water the garden, and there it divided and became four rivers. The name of the first is Pishon. It is the one that flows around the whole land of Havilah, where there is gold. And the gold of that land is good; bdellium and onyx stone are there. The name of the second river is Gihon. It is the one that flows around the whole land of Cush. And the name of the third river is the Tigris, which flows east of Assyria. And the fourth river is the Euphrates" (ESV).*

The Hebrew meaning of Pishon is "shaking the region; great diffusion, break apart or scatter; tear in pieces". The Hebrew meaning of Gihon is "bursting forth, gushing". These rivers are no longer visible but based on the descriptions, some scholars have placed Eden just east of Ethiopia also known as "Cush."

Why is this important? Because it is smack dab in the middle of Africa – which is generally accepted as the cradle of all civilization!

However, some authorities believe that because The Pishon and Gihon Rivers are no longer visible, it is impossible to locate The Garden of Eden. Fortunately, the *Book of Jubilees*[1] gives the precise location. Unfortunately, this particular source of information complicates things because most Christians are unfamiliar with the *Book of Jubilees*. In fact, many Christians have been forbidden to take anything from non-canonized text.

I want to interject that even though Jubilees was not part of the Canon, parts of the Book were discovered in the Dead Sea Scrolls.[2]

As a result of rejecting the *Book of Jubilees*, we have missed the revelation of relevant historical truths in God's Word. This information is critical to setting the factual context of the location of the Garden of Eden. Otherwise, it makes it easy to superimpose one's own beliefs into the two rivers' location. It also allows for the other two to be presupposed elsewhere.

---

1 The Book of Jubilees is canonized in the Ethiopian Orthodox Church and by Ethiopian Jews, but it is not part of the Canonized versions of the Christian Bibles. It does provide rich historical context that compliments the texts in the Christian Bible. However, it is not a part of the canonized (authorized) 66 Books of the Christian Bible.

2 Dead Sea Scrolls are ancient manuscripts written on papyrus paper that were found in caves in 1948 in Qumran. Many of these scrolls were still in a condition that their authenticity could be confirmed. Along with these manuscripts – original manuscripts of canonized texts were also found, including texts from parts of Isaiah. See section on the Apocrypha for more information.

You may be wondering why all this matters. It matters because it links to our historical Biblical ancestry that we will explore in the Book of Jubilees! Also keep in mind the definition of the Pishon River as it has significance in the narrative of God's chosen people.

Possible Location of the Garden of Eden

The Book of Jubilees gives the exact location of the Garden of Eden and information on Adam and Eve not found in the canonized version of the Bible.

We read in *The Ancient Book of Jubilees (Johnson, 2013):*

"And on the new moon of the fourth month,
Adam and his wife went forth from the Garden
of Eden and they dwelt in the land of Elda in
the land of their creation" (Jubilees 3:32).

Elda translates to Ethiopia. We also learn in Jubilees that Adam and Eve were in the Garden exactly seven years before God escorted them out, due to their disobedience against God. Their disobedience brought "sin" into the world. Prior to their disobedience, sin did not exist.

It is interesting to note the number seven in the Bible reflects spiritual completeness, the Father's perfection, and resurrection.

Now, let us look at the following description from the Book of Jubilees that pinpoints the exact location of the Garden of Eden.

"And he (Shem) knew that the garden of Eden is the Holy
of Hollies, and the dwelling place of the Lord, and Mount
Sinai, the center of the desert, and Mount Zion, the
center of the naval of the earth, these three, opposite one

another, were created as sanctuaries" (Jubilees 8:17).

The following map, developed by Chris Ward, (Ward, 1998) pinpoints the possible location of the Garden of Eden using an ancient method called triangulation and lines up with the description in the Book of Jubilees.

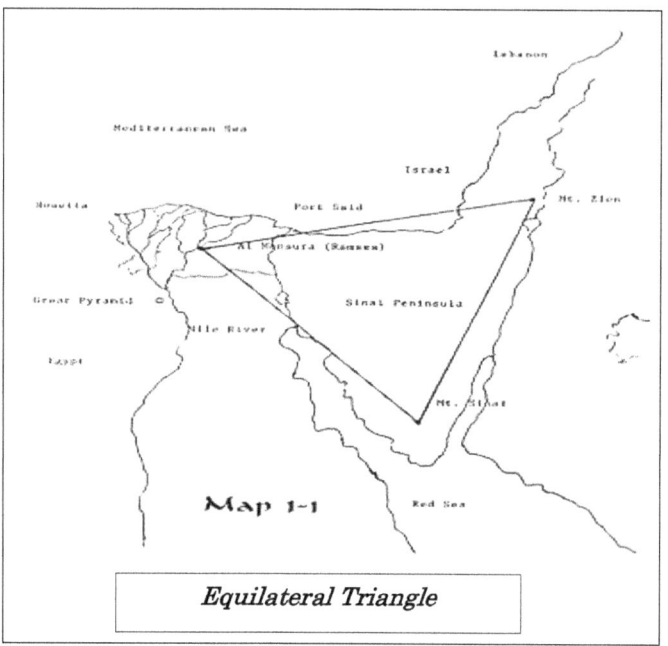

Map 1-1

Equilateral Triangle

The author of this Equilateral Triangle concludes; "...The most obvious conclusion is that the Garden of Eden was located in the Delta of the Nile River in the land of Goshen in Egypt (Ward, 1998)."

Egypt is in Africa

Ward also writes;

"The discovery of the location of the Garden of Eden also points to another significant and interesting fact. The Garden is located at '32 East by '32 North exactly in

the center of the land mass of the world (Ward, 1998)."

That is incredible! This information is one step closer to pulling back the layers of lies and deception that have otherwise been regarded as truth.

Credible resources and information are available today that give closer insight into information that has otherwise been unavailable for hundreds of years.

Have you ever put a jigsaw puzzle together to discover that a piece is missing? You have knowledge that it is missing, you can see that it is missing, but you do not know how it will blend once complete. The missing information made it extremely difficult to connect all the dots of our history.

Each writing, read, or studied on this subject adds a unique piece to the puzzle. Putting those pieces together takes time and effort. Remember, sometimes those pieces will not fit properly; no matter how hard you shove them into place just to be done with it – it never works. You cannot force it. If you do, it will be visible to the discerning eye, defacing the value of the entire puzzle.

Therefore, the search must continue until the full puzzle on the full revelation of this truth to the African American's Ancestry is revealed and properly fits in place.

REFLECTIONS

CHAPTER TWO

NEGROLAND

"Negroland" – was a term coined by European mapmakers to designate an area in Africa inhabited by dark-skinned people. Although this area had not been fully explored or widely known to colonizers, the name, *"Negroland"* was implemented somewhere after 1675 and placed on the map in 1710. The boundaries drawn by the trusted, well-known mapmaker were to distinguish the differences in the cultural behaviors of the dark-skinned people they encountered. The Israelites migrated to this region after the fall of Jerusalem in 70 A.D. Ethiopia is also in this region (pictured at end of the Chapter).

In another map from the year 1600 (also pictured at the end of the Chapter) you will find in that area a region titled, Nigritie.

Be aware that when you view maps by various map makers of that time, you will see variations.

In the book, *"100 Amazing Facts About the Negro with Complete Proof"* (Rodgers, 1957), the author writes that the word Negro is one of the most ancient names for so-called

Black people and is a derivative from the River Niger in Africa. He asserts the word "Niger" found its way into the Latin culture. Since the people from that region were dark-skinned, Niger, Nigra and Nigrum came to mean Black, following the Latin definition. He adds that Negrito and Nigritia, mean "The people of the Great River." He also states, Negrito and Nigritia are from West Africa. Thus, the etymology of the word Negro was rendered Latin, but Latin is not it's true origin.

By not realizing the significance of what we discovered about ourselves as "Negros"; based on the Latin definition meaning "black in color;" the so-called "Negroes" in America rejected the title. Likewise, the slaves in America, who were called Black would have rejected or ignored the title because it did not reflect who they were. Consequently, their true identity would get lost in translations and changing of maps.

Herman Moll removed the title "Negroland" from his maps from what I can find after 1746.

Perhaps, what needs to be realized is that Black is not a race or nationality. It is a color. The title of Negro is actually more of a true identifier to our ancestry in Africa. If we knew that Negro referred to a people from a region of the Great River (Niger), that would certainly give more substance to an identity or at least a starting point to discover one's ancestry.

To say a person is Black, then ask where did they originate? Ok somewhere in Africa may be a response. But Africa is huge!

Now, through our ignorance and indoctrination we have reverted back to being called Black, which is a stumbling block to identifying our heritage.

Go to Africa and ask, who are the Black race and see how far you get! Good luck with that!

The slaves would have known Ethiopia, or Niger, but not necessarily Negroland because it was a fictitious name made up for the easy identification of human cargo thieves. Nevertheless, the name flourished and persevered as the region's original name even after disappearing from modern-day maps.

If someone were to do a current search for "Negroland," they could only locate it using an ancient map. Looking at such a map unaccompanied by the historical background, could lead one to believe it was an actual title and place. The significance, however, is that the region titled as such identifies a group of people by their heritage. A heritage that was subsequently drowned when ships sailed Negros across the sea as human cargo to a new land.

There is a book entitled, *"The Negroes in Negroland; The Negroes in America; and Negroes Generally"*, that was published in 1808, resurrected in 2017, and put back into print as a *Classic Reprint Series*. The book comprises excerpts from explorers who wrote about their experiences in Africa and with the people. The accounts are obscenely negative and possibly propaganda to justify enslavement and reinforce lies. The book can be considered disgusting at best.

It does; however, explain where some prevalent views of so-called African-Americans came from. For that reason alone, I will bring a few of them into our discussion. I read through the book and just highlighted certain words that were used throughout to describe black people in Africa:

> *"Faithless, cannibals, shameless beggars, savage, immoral, indecent, chastity unknown, superstitious, human butchers, prostitute, thief, drunkards, barbarism, these people, women exceedingly dirty."*

Many of these names are still used today; particularly: "those people, thief, dirty and savage".

This became the view of "ALL" dark-skinned people in Africa and was passed down to the New World. The significance of bringing this to light is to give insight into how these terms have become a standard description for African Americans. To combat this, we must know where it initiated and remove the easily adaptable descriptions placed upon African Americans.

Here are a few excerpts from this resurrected foolishness:

"I found that every Christian negress was a prostitute and that every Christian negro was a thief."

Note how they identify these "black" Christians – as prostitutes and thieves. That is deep!

"The Negress has beauty, beauty despite her black skin, which might create a furor in our demi-monde*1, and for which fools might fling their fortunes to the dogs. And she is gentle and faithful, and loving in her own poor way. But where is the coy glance, the tender sigh, the timid blush? Where is the intellect, which is the light within the crystal lamp, the genius within the clay? No, no, the negress is not a woman, she is a parody of woman; she is a pretty toy, an affectionate brute, - that is all."

Aside from being utterly ridiculous, this particular statement is contradictory at best. First, it says the Negress is gentle, faithful, and loving. Then it says she has no intellect and is not a woman at all. Does the definition depend on what the expectation of the woman is at a particular time?

---

1 *Demimonde - The class of women considered to be of doubtful morality and social standing (Merriam-Webster Dictionary).

A: a class of women on the fringes of respectable society supported by wealthy lovers; also: their world B: the world of prostitution.

B: a distinct circle or world that is often an isolated part of a larger world a night in the disco demimonde; especially: one having low reputation or prestige (Merriam-Webster Dictionary).

*"The negro is a being who invents nothing, originates
nothing, improves nothing; who can only cook,
nurse, and fiddle; who has neither energy nor
industry, save in rare cases, that prove the rule; ..."*

We know this to be quite the opposite. Many inventions of "black-skinned" people have made it into history books. The Egyptians, who were originally black-skinned, were brilliant inventors of, medically, scientifically, and mathematically advanced societies.

*"The slave in Louisiana had become free, de facto,
and in a qualified sense; but, alas? His freedom only
meant the power to become idle, to become immoral,
to sicken and to die." (The Negroes in Negroland; The
Negroes in America; and the Negroes Generally, 1808)."*

If this is one's view, certainly, there is nothing wrong with enslavement and the use of chains to tame the beasts! While I will not highlight any additional excerpts from this obscene falsehood, we must begin to get to the bottom of where this madness started.

We must turn this around with our upcoming generation and begin to teach our children and children's children the truth about who they are – of who we are. We must counteract it with the awesome truth that catapults them into a state of reality, increasing their self-esteem and worthiness through a true identity of who they are.

We must highlight the contributions the so-called African Americans have made to the world and continue teaching about the countless inventions they made. We must affirm our brilliant minds, faithfulness, forgiving nature, and giving hearts. Yes – we are a special people – but not in the way perceived by this country and the world for over 400 years.

It is time to awaken our consciousness with the richness of the royalty within us – and not in the sense of arrogance or returning to a state of idolatrous living – but to truly live as we have been created and set apart to do.

We must dig deep into the craters of lies that we have accepted as truth for over 400 years and begin to look at ourselves, considering who we truly are. We have an identity that we have denied and has been denied to us ancestrally, historically, and literally.

We have allowed ourselves to be disconnected from our true identity and have accepted the identity imposed or beaten upon us when we were exiled into this land called America.

We need to understand who we truly are to understand God's original plan and purpose for our lives and live it.

We must return to God collectively – because we are a collective group of people. Think about it, we have dreamed, pledged to keep hope alive, intellectualized, theorized, and spiritualized. We have marched by the millions, cast out demons by the billions, and kept it real, but have failed to collectively make any major strides in the wholistic deliverance of our people. It is time for a collective revival.

I envision a unified day of prayer across this nation, expanding globally with hands, hearts, voices, and minds linked in repentance. Through these prayers for our people, our cities, our nation and one another, our breakthrough will manifest.

I envision backs straightening, individuals and families restored, faith at work, love of self-personified, and a unified community at hand reach.

Listen to the words in Jeremiah 18:21:

"So give their children over to famine; hand them over to the power of the sword. Let their wives be made childless and widows; let their men be put to death, their young men slain by the sword in battle" (NIV).

This should bring chills to your spine or, more appropriately, drop you to your knees in prayer. Our children are dying of gun violence, and we have the highest rate in the nation of single-mother homes. Our men and increasingly more women are in prison in alarming numbers. Our young men are killing each other ruthlessly!

Only God can fix this – but we must seek Him. We cannot run and hide from it – we cannot disassociate ourselves from it – because it is us – they are us, and we are them! It was prophesied, *"We are our brother's keeper."* Prayer costs us nothing, yet repays bountifully.

Negroland was the fictitious title of a region in Africa. By highlighting this area on a map, it pinpointed to the explorers the desired captives.

This hand-picked group of people, (Hebrews) were classified as refined and intelligent, by the explorers. Yet they were sold as slaves in a land beyond the waters; labeled, brutalized, stripped of their identity – given a new identity – and tasked with building a nation they were never accepted or treated with a sense of dignity in.

It is time to permanently leave "Negroland" and remove the resulting residue it has left on the African American community. It is time that we redefine who we are – based on the Word of God.

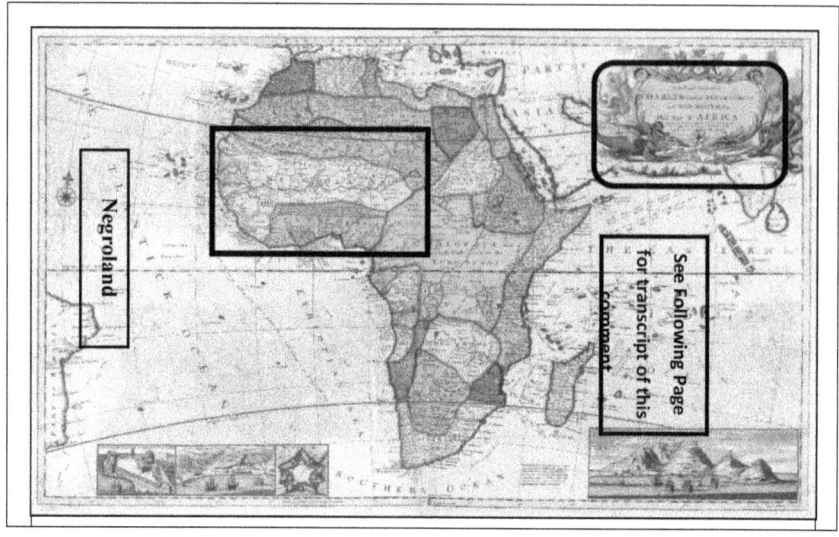

"Herman Moll (c. 1654-1732) was one of the most important London mapmakers in the first half of the eighteenth century. Most of Niger River watershed is termed "Negroland", a term which Moll helped establish in 18th century English mapmaking."

Transcript of Comments on the Negroland Map:

"I am credibly informed that y country about hundred leagues north of the Coast of Guinea is (un)inhabited by white men, or at least a different kind of people from the Blacks, who wear cloaths, and have use of letters, make silk, & that some of them keep the Christian Sabbath."

Comment on Ethiopia:

"Country is wholly unknown to the Europeans."
--Geographer H. Moll for Charles Earl of Peterborough and Monmouth

Map of 1710 by a Different Map Maker
(Unknown, 2020)

*Notice the area circled says Nigritie and not Negroland. The small circle identifies the Kingdom of Judah (spelled Juda).

REFLECTIONS

CHAPTER THREE

DNA Evidence

W hat is **DNA**? DNA (Deoxyribonucleic acid) is a molecular genetic code within our bodies that uniquely identifies every person. It is used to find parents, solve crimes, identify people, and in very recent years, trace a person's ancestral lineage.

I had a DNA test done on my dad, showing his largest concentration of genetic markers are from Nigeria (Negroland). I must admit, I was very disillusioned after learning that 99% of African Americans were rooted back in the western region of Africa. Since then, I have come to understand how a large section of western Africa was designated as Negroland. What was once of disinterest has become critically significant.

The slave trade was primarily launched from the West Coast of Africa. That is why 99% of our DNA comes from that region. Subsequently, I had a genetics test done on myself. The highest percentage of my African genetic markers is from the Yoruba people in Nigeria, followed by the Ivory Coast and Ghana, all within West Africa.

There was a study done in 1999 by a French historian, named Tudor Parfitt. He became aware of a tribe in Africa called the Lemba. The Lemba still practiced Old Testament laws and customs. When asked, they said they were descendants of the Biblical Levite Priest, Aaron. Yes, Aaron - the brother of Moses, that Biblical emancipator of Egyptian slavery. A DNA analysis was conducted and came back **confirming** they are, in fact, descendants of Aaron.[1]

The Levite Tribe was selected and set apart by God as the Priesthood. They had a different and distinct DNA Chromosomal characteristic than the other Tribes of Israel. The Lemba tribe has this same distinctive chromosomal characteristic in their DNA. This information was obtained from some of my earliest ventures into this study. I had knowledge without understanding at that time. I was still excited, to say the least – but it wasn't until I learned the differences in the Tribes of the Israelites that it began to sink in.

Read carefully the following quote regarding this discovery from The World Jewish Congress:

"Genetic tests carried out by British scientists have revealed that many of the Lemba tribesmen in southern Africa have Jewish origins, according to a report by the BBC (British Broadcasting Corporation). The Lemba, a tribe of 70,000 to 80,000 members who live in central Zimbabwe and northern South Africa, have customs similar to Jewish ones: Lemba refrain from eating pork or other foods forbidden by the Torah, or forbidden combinations of permitted foods.

---

1 Tudor Parfitt's original findings appear to have been watered down over the years. In his writings in 1999, he concluded that the Y Chromosome found in the Lemba people was rare, distinctly, and uniquely found in the Levites. Updated efforts have been made to resolve this as oral tradition, and complicated scientific studies, to disprove the original findings.

They wear yarmulke-like skull caps, conduct ritual animal slaughter, and have a holy day once a week. They even put a Star of David on their gravestones. According to their oral tradition, the Lemba are descended from seven Jewish men who left Israel 2,500 years ago and married African women, according to the BBC. The Lemba prefer their children to marry other Lembas', and marriage to non-Lembas' is discouraged.

Their sacred prayer language is a mixture of Hebrew and Arabic. Their religious artifact is a replica of the Biblical Ark of the Covenant known as the 'Ngoma lungundu', meaning "the drum that thunders." The object went on display recently at a museum in Harare, Zimbabwe, which instilled pride in many of the Lemba. They say the ark was built almost 700 years ago from the remains of the original ark, which according to the Bible, was used to store the Ten Commandments. The ancient vessel was thought to be lost for decades until it was recently discovered in a storeroom in Harare.

The members of the priestly clan of Lemba, called the Buba – which is one of 12 clans – have a genetic element also found among the Jewish priestly line, known as Kohanim. 'This was amazing,' Professor Tudor Parfitt from the University of London told the BBC; 'It looks as if the Jewish priesthood continued in the West by people called Cohen, and in the same way it was continued by the priestly clan of the Lemba' (World Jewish Congress, 2010)."

Lemba Leaders/Priests [2]

An article in the *New York Times*, written closer to the time of the original study concludes the following from Tudor Parfitt:

> *"But the remarkable thing about the Lemba tradition is that it may be exactly right. A team of geneticists has found that many Lemba men carry in their male chromosome a set of DNA sequences that is distinctive of the Cohanim, the Jewish priests believed to be the descendants of Aaron. The genetic signature of priests -- a hereditary caste, different from rabbis but with certain ritual roles -- is particularly common among Lemba men who belong to the senior of their 12 groups, known as the Buba clan (Wade, 1999)."*

The article further states:

> *"The mutations are particularly helpful for reconstructing population history because each lineage of men has its own distinctive pattern of mutations. It was a Y chromosome study last year that confirmed the oral tradition among the descendants of the slave Sally Hemings that their ancestor was Thomas Jefferson (Wade, 1999)."*

---

2 Photo of Lemba Priests/Leaders (World Jewish Congress, 2010).

A more widely known tribe in Africa, called The Ashanti, has some of the same similarities as the Buba and Cohen. I am unaware of any DNA testing, but they have also been linked to the original Hebrews. They have maintained their heritage through oral teachings, historical knowledge, and the continuation of rituals as described in the Old Testament.

The tribal name, Ashanti, gives continued knowledge, of their heritage and identity as follows; Ashan was the name of a city in Judah's regional territory, and Ti means the people of. If we put them together, it means the people of Ashan. They know who they are and have not allowed their identity to be stripped away.

A modern-day Tribe – the Falasha, has been relocating to Jerusalem for some years now. However, to live there, they had to prove Ancestral lineage. Once their heritage was confirmed, they were allowed to move back, but were allegedly treated as second and third class citizens. The women were also allegedly being sterilized without their knowledge. The irony is the land belongs to them. They are not the foreigners – they are the rightful owner. Indeed, DNA has advanced society to use "scientific" methods to prove or disprove information. It is amazing to me how God has wired the human body. Scientists can utilize the data that was already existent in the beginning. God knew what it would take to reveal the truth, and he has used science as a means for man to believe he has discovered something new! The Bible tells us there is nothing new under the sun. Man may discover, but God created, and He has used science to push his truth forward to a disbelieving and discrediting world.

Could this be one of the reasons we find science being attacked today? We love science when it lines up to man's desires and disregard it when it points to God.

REFLECTIONS

CHAPTER FOUR

GENEALOGY: HAMITES VS. SHEMITES

t has been my experience in Biblical teaching that the so called "Black" race are descendants of Noah's son Ham. Well, if the explorers could make up a location and rename the people, they could also make up their ancestry! The thought being everyone who is black are descendants of Ham. That is not wholistically true. The so-called African-Americans are actually descendants of Noah's son Shem. If you do not get anything else in this book, get this revelation – because it is the truth that will set you free.

This is the big lie that was used to justify slavery.

In order to understand the story of Noah's sons, let us journey back to Genesis Chapters 9 and 10. Noah had three sons. Japheth, Shem and Ham.

Ham found his father lying naked in bed following a night of drinking wine from his vineyard. Instead of respecting his father, he mocked him and brought his brothers to see him in that state. According to Genesis in the Christian Bible, when Noah awoke from his drunken stupor and discovered what Ham had done, he cursed Ham's offspring saying they would be slaves (servants) to their brothers. Ham's descendants (Canaan) were cursed because of Ham's **sin,** not his skin (Genesis 9:22), which was the justification for enslaving a specific, black-skinned segment of society.

Now, let us consider the justification for enslavement being the color of his skin. Does that not indicate he was other than white, and they knew it? He was "black-skinned" – full stop. Based on their own justification for slavery in America, from this very text in Genesis, dark-skinned people were known in the beginning, because "Genesis" means beginning. There is also a recent suggestion that Canaan (Ham's son) defied Noah's division of the land when he divided the land out to his sons. Thus, it was more about his disobedience, than the mockery of his grandfather, Noah. In either case, it had nothing to do with skin tone or color. This has been a perverted teaching of scripture.

For the sake of clarity, African Americans are from the tribe of Judah. Judah is a descendant of Shem. Judah follows the line of the ancestral promise God gave to the Hebrew people. Just like the Levites were set aside for the priesthood, Judah was set aside as the Hebrews.

All Israelites are not Hebrews. But all fall under the umbrella of the Nation of Israel through the twelve tribes.

The Hamites assisted with the slave trade to sell the Shemites into slavery. It was the Hamites who were considered by the explorers at the time to be unrefined. If you flip back to the map of Negroland, you will see this comment with the distinction of the different Black people the explorers encountered. I am not saying or suggesting the explorers were accurate in their description. It is how "they" chose to distinguish the differences in the cultures "they" allegedly observed.

The Shemites were cultural and intelligent. They were skilled in agriculture. And guess what? Was that not one of the most used skills in the U.S. during slavery?

Examine *Zondervan's Compact Bible Dictionary* definition of Ham. *"Ham: The youngest son of Noah, born probably about 96 years before the Flood, and one of the eight persons to live through the Flood. He became a progenitor of the dark races, not the Negros [Hebrews], but the Egyptians, Ethiopians, Libyans, Canaanites"* (Douglas & Tenney, 1987). Upon close examination of this definition, it confirms that Shem and Ham were both black or dark-skinned nations. Ham's descendants were black, but not Hebrew.

Shem is the ancestor of the Hebrew people, while Ham is the ancestor of the African people. Both are Black! However, there are distinct biblical and cultural differences between the two. Japheth was the ancestor of the European race. These distinctions between the two dark-skinned cultures are noted on the maps. By modern-day definition, African Americans are from the ancestral line of Shem – the Lion of the Tribe of Judah – God's chosen people. It does not take much imagination to consider why we were stripped of this identity – but it will take a miracle to accept it universally.

The good news is, God is still in the miracle-working, promise-keeping business.

REFLECTIONS

_____

_____

_____

_____

_____

_____

_____

_____

_____

_____

_____

_____

_____

_____

_____

_____

_____

_____

_____

_____

_____

_____

_____

_____

_____

_____

_____

_____

_____

CHAPTER FIVE

THE TRIBE OF JUDAH

Who was Judah?

We have already established that Noah had three sons: Japheth, Shem and Ham. Judah is a descendant of Shem, Noah's middle son. He is the fourth son of Jacob with his first wife Leah. He was the head of one of the 12 Tribes of Israel – The Tribe of Judah.

The Tribe of Judah was a very powerful, if not *the most* powerful Tribe in early Israel's history. The Bible mentions their strength, but other historical writings also mention their vast acts of power.

The ancestral lineage is paramount here. It is from the line of Shem that the Messiah (Christ) was prophesied to come. It is from The Tribe of Judah (descendant of Shem) that African Americans and others descended from.

Let us first look at the blessing and prophecy concerning Judah bestowed upon him by his father Jacob.

In Genesis 49:8-10 we read;

"Judah, your brothers shall praise you; your hand shall be on the neck of your enemies; your father's sons shall bow down before you. Judah is a lion's cub; from the prey, my son, you have gone up. He stooped down; he crouched as a lion and as a lioness; who dares rouse him? The scepter shall not depart from Judah nor the ruler's staff from between his feet, until tribute comes to him; and to him shall be the obedience of the peoples" (ESV).

The scepter was a rod that a king held to symbolize his authority. In Hebrew, the word scepter means rod, staff, branch, offshoot, or tribe. The relevance here is that Judah's branch would have leadership. We see this in the history of King David.

King David was a descendent of Judah and the first earthly king crowned from this lineage. Jesus, the everlasting, perpetual king, is a descendant of David.

In the New Testament we read in Hebrews 7:14:

"For it is evident that our Lord was descended from Judah..." (ESV).

The scripture emphasizes that the Bible is a continuous story. The lineage of Judah begins in the Old Testament. [The book of Hebrews is in the New Testament.]

For a quick and easy snapshot, the following graphic is a very high-level genealogical line of some more commonly known names in the line of Shem that links to Jesus.

Noah Line

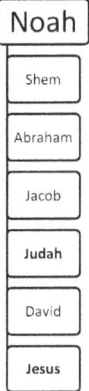

Take a close look at the map below showing where the Kingdom of Judah was located in 1747. You will find the words, "K of Juda" by the phrase "Slave Coast" just below the area identified as "Negroland". It was eventually removed, potentially wiping out Judah's history. However, removing Judah from the face of the map, did not wipe the Hebrews off the face of the earth! They were just relocated.

Negroland Map

Let us examine some written texts about Judah and the Israelites' extraordinary strength and physical power. Writings are presented from both Biblical and non-Biblical historical reports.

These historical writings detail the Hebrew's great and supernatural strength and abilities, recording events in which they wiped out armies and how they were greatly feared. The fear was not just because of their strength, but it was also recognized by their adversaries that God was with them. They were fearless in their fighting, and it was well known not to do battle with them without the assistance of other armies.

Judah is said to have had even more exceptional strength and supernatural power than his brothers, especially in war. Get your popcorn! This is good. If nothing else, it will make for a great movie!

From the Book of Jasher, we read:

> "...and Judah was jealous of his God in this matter, and he called out and said, O Lord, help, send help to us and our brothers. And he ran at a distance with all his might, with his drawn sword in his hand, and he sprang from the earth and by dint of his strength, mounted the wall, and his sword fell from his hand. And Judah shouted upon the wall, and all the men that were upon the wall were terrified, and some of them fell from the wall into the city and died, and those who were yet upon the wall when they saw Judah's strength, they were greatly afraid and fled for their lives into the city for safety" (Jasher 39:28[b]-30).

We also find in Jasher a fascinating and compelling showdown between Joseph and Judah when the sons of Jacob (Joseph's brothers) made a second journey to Egypt to purchase food during a severe famine in their land.

On their first trip to Egypt, Joseph accused them of being spies and held one brother (Simeon) back, under the pretense of collateral. They were told with very clear instructions that when they returned to Egypt, they were to bring Benjamin, their youngest brother with them. Benjamin was Joseph's only full brother.

When their first food supply ran out, it became necessary for them to return to Egypt to survive the famine. Judah convinces Jacob they must do as instructed on the first visit and bring Benjamin with them. He gives his word to Jacob that he would carry the burden of guilt for the rest of his life if he did not return with Benjamin. Jacob reluctantly gives in, and they return to Egypt with Benjamin.

When they arrived with Benjamin as instructed, Joseph still gave them a hard time. He released Simeon but refused to release Benjamin. At this point, the warrior in Judah arose, and the lion in him came out.

Judah bursts through a closed door to confront Joseph, and the two become engaged in a heated and loud argument. They each make harrowing threats of harm against one another and demonstrate some of the extraordinary powers they possess.

Trash-talking is apparently an inherited trait for African Americans!

This conversation is not found in the Christian Bible. It reads in part:

> *"And when Judah heard this thing, he was exceedingly wroth and his anger burned within him, and there was before him in that place a stone, the weight of which was about four hundred shekels[1], and Judah's anger was kindled, and he took the stone in one hand and cast it to the heavens and caught it with his left hand. And he placed it afterward under his legs, and he sat upon it with all his strength and the stone was turned into dust from the force of Judah."*

---

1 400 Shekels = 10 pounds.

"And Joseph saw the act of Judah and he was very much afraid, but he commanded Manasseh his son and he also did with another stone like unto the act of Judah, and Judah said unto his brethren, let not any of you say this man is an Egyptian, but by his doing this thing he is of our father's family" (Jasher 54:27-30).

In this small portion of the narrative, Judah and Joseph recognized one another's leadership, physical strength, and power. Keep in mind Judah was Joseph's older brother, and Joseph knew who Judah was, but Judah did not know who Joseph was other than second in command to Pharoah.

Let us set the contextual background for understanding how Judah would not have recognized his younger brother. When Joseph was young, his brothers were jealous of him. During that time his siblings were out working in the field. It was getting late in the day, and Jacob (their father) was concerned because they had not returned home yet. He sends Joseph to look for them.

His brothers see him coming from a distance and devise a plot to kill him. One brother convinces the others to put him in a cistern[2] instead of killing him, secretly planning to go back and rescue him later. So, they stripped him of the custom-made coat his father Jacob had given him, and then dropped him into a dried-out cistern. Their plan was to leave him in this deep/dark, snake infested hole in the ground, knowing that he could not climb out without assistance. And without water in it, survival was not possible.

Judah then speaks up and asks his brothers what they will gain from his death – knowing that Joseph would surely die in that pit. He then suggested selling him to some merchants on the road instead. The brothers agreed, pulled Joseph back out of the cistern and sold him into slavery to the merchants for

---

2 A cistern was a pit deep in the ground that stored water.

eight ounces of silver. The merchants took Joseph to Egypt and sold him to one of Pharaoh's officials.

The plot thickens. When the brothers return home without Joseph, who was sent to find them, they tell their father, Jacob, that Joseph was devoured by a beast and was dead. To convince their father of this lie, they presented Jacob with Joseph's blood-stained coat. The coat contained blood from an animal they killed to legitimize their story. As a result of this lie, Jacob fell into a deep state of grief and protective mode of his youngest son Benjamin.

Fast forward several years later, they did not recognize their brother when they had to journey to Egypt for food during a severe drought. He was in his younger stage of life when they last saw him. Now he is *the man* in Egypt with power and authority, presumably an Egyptian.

The exchange between Joseph and Judah is compelling because Joseph recognizes his brother's supernatural strength and power. Judah, on the other hand, did not recognize Joseph. However, he recognized the strength of his nephew, Manasseh, because it was unmatched by anyone other than the Twelve Tribes of Israel. Judah then says:

"this man is not an Egyptian; he is of our father's family."

Which narrows that down to being his close relative.

There were several extraordinary acts of power displayed between the two during this time, as well as threats.

It is also noted that when Joseph imprisoned Simeon, Manasseh knocked him down by striking him over the back of his neck. Simeon made a similar comment:

"This blow was not dealt by an Egyptian,
but by one belonging to our house."

These statements certainly make one wonder if Judah also became fearful or convicted by a flashback of what he and his brothers did to Joseph years ago.

He knew Joseph had not been killed. Yet when he is on the verge of rage, he realizes after he threatens this "Egyptian" to wipe out all of Egypt, that something else is happening here. There was a serious power play between two powerful leaders.

Judah was second in command to Jacob. Joseph was second in command to Pharoah. One unto God and one unto man, which is so applicable to life today! It poses the question, under whose power and authority are you living?

Even Joseph, with his full earthly power, was initially fearful of his brother. He knew that the power of Judah was of God, and the power of Egypt was of man. He eventually stopped the showdown by acknowledging to his brothers that he was Joseph.

From *The Legends of the Jews Complete* (Ginzberg) consider the following excerpts highlighting the strength of Judah:

"Girt with his sword, Jacob advanced against the enemy,
and in the first onslaught he slew twelve thousand of
the weak in the army. Then Judah spake to him, and
said, 'Father, thou are tired and exhausted, let me fight
the enemy alone.' And Jacob replied saying, 'Judah,
my son, I know thy strength and thy bravery, that they
are exceeding great so that none in the world is like
unto thee therein.' His countenance like a lion's and
inflamed with wrath, Judah attacked the army, and
slew twelve myriads[3] of tried and famous warriors."

---

3 One Myriad = 10,000. Hence according to this account that would make it 120,000.

*"When the warriors caught sight of Judah's lion
face and his lion teeth, and heard his lion voice,
they were greatly afraid. Judah hopped and jumped
over the army like a flea, from one warrior to the
next raining blows down upon them incessantly,
and by evening he had slain eighty thousand and
ninety-six men, armed with swords and bows."*

*"Then Judah's towering rage began to show
signs of breaking out; his right eye shed tears of
blood; the hair above his heart grew so stiff that
it pierced and rent the five garments in which he
was clothed; and he took brass rods, bit them with
his teeth and spat them out as fine powder."*

We read in 1 Chronicles 5:2:

*"...though Judah was the strongest of his
brothers and a ruler came from him, the rights
of the firstborn belonged to Joseph" (NIV).*

Revelation 5:5 reads:

*"And one of the elders said to me, Weep no
more, behold, the Lion of the tribe of Judah, the
Root of David, has conquered, so that he can
open the scroll and its seven seals" (ESV).*

The scepter has been passed on to Christ – through his lineage in David. I cannot help but wonder if this fits into the fear factor that some other nations have about African Americans, particularly African American men. While this information has been hidden – and though it was not readily accessible - it does and always did exist.

There are so many stigmas, and fears that appear to be unwarranted from the perspective of African Americans.

Unwarranted from not understanding the pit from which they were birthed.

What we see coming to the light is a possible basis for some of these fears and stigmas. They were deeply rooted and buried in the annals of historical data we have not previously been privy to. African Americans may have not known, but someone did!

For the record, women were also brave and fought in battles when required. Is this the root of the strength of the so-called African American woman as well?

The Hebrews were always at war – with their enemies, including their kin. The truth of the matter is – we will continue to be at war until Jesus returns.

Various Views and Breakdowns of Hebrew Dispersions

GENEALOGICAL SKETCH CHART OF ISRAEL

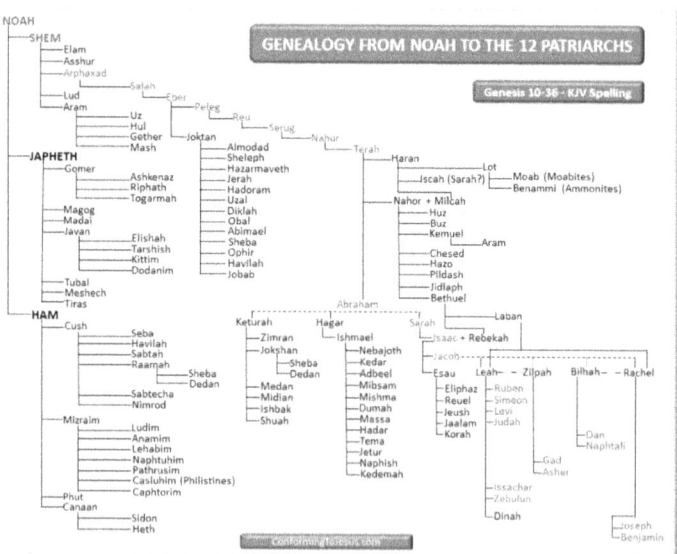

NATION OF ISRAEL   ## HAM/SHEM MAP

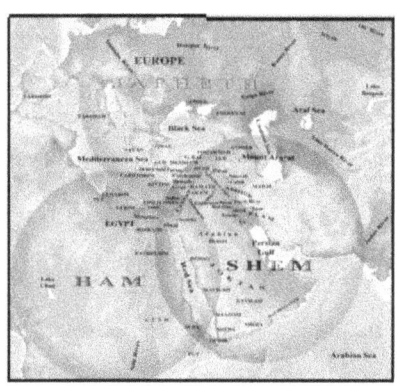

NATION OF ISRAEL

JUDAH NEGROES OF
AMERICA, UK, CANADA, PANAMA, SOUTH AMERICA
Dimona Israel - JAMAICANS, HAITIANS, CUBA - NEGROES
OUT OF ALL NATION
ISRAELITES/ NEGROID RACE OF ZULU/GAD OF SOUTH
AFRICA, -IBO'S / JUDAH OF NIGERIA ASHANTI'S OF
GHANA -YORUBA'S OF NIGERIA MANDINGO'S -TEMME
KRIO'S FULANI AND MENDE OF SIERRA
LEONE EWE TRIBE OF NIGERIA AND TOGO WOLOF
TRIBE OF SENEGAL
BAMILEKE TRIBE GA,FANTI,SEEWI TRIBES OF GHANA-
LEMBA LEVI OF SOUTH AFRICA -Haussa / Issachar,
OF Cameroon ,NEGROES OF THE CONGO,

THE LIST GOES ON FOR THE NEGRO RACE,
THE TRUE CHILDREN OF IS RA EL, BY
THE BLOOD LINE A GENETIC AND BIBLICAL
HISTORICAL FACT....

THEE NEGRO RACE

RACIAL ORIGINS
TRACED FROM NOAH

Shem	Ham	Japheth
Jews	African races	Western Europeans
Semitic people	Canaanite nations	Caucasians
Oriental races		

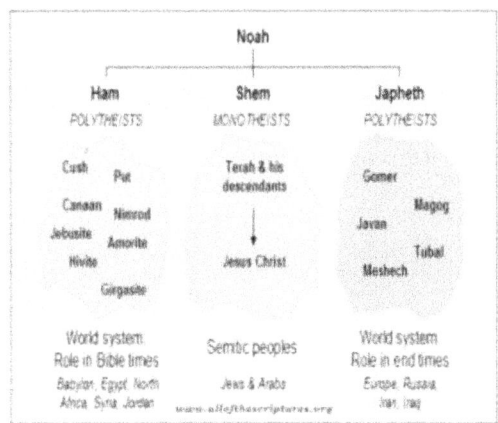

TWELVE TRIBES OF ISRAEL

	Tribe	Dispersion*8	Blessing	Curse	Character Trait
1.	Judah (Praised)	African Americans in America	Messiah/Christ Leadership Strength Power Wisdom Knowledge	Slavery	Money Conscious Drunkenness Greed
2.	Levi (Joined To)	Haitians	Priesthood Understanding	Anger	Cruel
3.	Reuben (Behold a Son)	Seminole Indians	First Born – Sign of strength, excelled in power and honor.	Power removed	Unstable Fornication
4.	Simeon (Heard)	Dominicans		Anger	Cruel Jealousy
5.	Issachar (There is Recompense)	Mexicans	Strong Good and fertile land.		Integrity
6.	Zebulun (Exalted)	Guatemala to Panama	No Sickness or Disease Dwelling at seashore/haven for ships.		Compassionate to Poor Generous
7.	Dan (Judge)		Judge		Envy Boastful Anger Liar
8.	Naphtali (Wrestling)	Argentina to Chile	Dove Exceedingly Swift		
9.	Gad (Troop)	North American Indians	Died in Peace while still vigorous.		Hatred
10.	Asher (Happy)	Columbia to Uruguay	Blessed/Chef		
11.	Joseph (Jehovah has Added)	Sons: Ephraim Puerto Rico Manasseh Cuba	Fruitful Leader Powerful		Integrity
12.	Benjamin (Son of the Right Hand)	West Indians	Lived a long life Died Peaceful		Wolf

R E F L E C T I O N S

_____

_____

_____

_____

_____

_____

CHAPTER SIX

Introduction to the Books of the Apocrypha

There is an opportunity for open and honest discussions and, more importantly – seeking God's wisdom and instruction regarding the Apocryphal Books of the Bible. What is the Apocrypha? The word *Apocrypha* means hidden or secret. The Apocrypha consists of Biblical writings that were not canonized or approved as authentic for inclusion in the Christian Bible. The 66 Books in the Christian Bible represent what is called the Canon of Scripture. The Catholic and Ethiopian Bibles, however, carry fifteen Apocrypha books in addition to the Canon.

What does it mean to be canonized? The text had to pass a rigorous test to be considered an authoritative – divinely inspired writing of God. 2 Timothy 3:16 teaches that:

"All Scripture is breathed out by God..." (ESV).

There were thoughts and reasons behind the decision to reject the texts.

Some manuscripts were deemed to have not been written in a time frame consistent with the original writing – meaning they were written far afterward or copied – or the source needed to be deemed dependable or divinely inspired. Furthermore, copies were produced by hand and included the translation of texts from original Hebrew to Greek and Latin. The hand-written copies did not result in exact replicas of the original source.

After Christs' death, numerous teachings were adopted, much of which was heresy. To bring teachings back to the authenticity of original manuscripts, a counsel of church scholars and elders convened at what was called the Council of Nicaea.

If you have ever heard the Nicene Creed, it was written as a universal Christian statement of faith and belief in the Holy Scriptures.

The Apocrypha was included in the first 200 years of the authorized version of the Christian Bible.

Even from my late teenage years, I had an inner drive to gain a deeper understanding of the Bible. This craving caused me to read the Apocrypha in the Catholic Bible. I was intrigued, to say the least, and it kept my mind inquisitive about the stories within.

However, it was an independent endeavor with the exception and prompting of the Holy Spirit, who was with me, but whom I did not personally know at that time. My mother encouraged me to read it – based on the interest I expressed to her. I believe she bought the Catholic Bible, which gave me knowledge of the existence of these writings, but that was the extent of it.

My Christian background taught me that "I should not take or even read the Apocrypha because it was all heresy and detrimental to my faith." Additionally, I should only consider the writings as interesting stories. While I subscribed to that prevalent teaching, at least in my small world of theological resources – I did just that. I read it as though it were a Christian novel. However, deep in my soul – I felt there was more. My spirit did not let me completely drop the desire to gain a deeper understanding. I continued to press and stumble my way through, remarking the stories as very interesting, even sharing when I had an opportunity with anyone who had a listening ear.

I wondered why one group of Christians accepted it as an additional text, and others banned it as heresy? Why were they preserved at all if it were not at the hand of God? How do we reconcile the findings of some of these writings in the Dead Sea Scrolls? Many of which have been authenticated and preserved for over a thousand years. If you desire to dig deeper to uncover the hidden identity of African Americans, then it is imperative that you read them.

To African Americans, once you begin to read and God opens your mind to the knowledge and understanding of who you are, Negroland will be forever buried. African Americans, your Hebrew heritage is real.

African Americans will understand the judgment they are under, their part in being exiled, but more importantly, their rightful place in this life and the one to come.

 It is no accident these hidden, secret, and banned books from the Bible have been resurfacing. It is no accident that what they reveal is liberating – in the sense of identity. It is no wonder they were not even included in the "approved" Apocrypha but hidden and buried even deeper.

The additional information one gains when given a clearer understanding of the Bible is amazing. Not to mention the shedding of light on a people called "peculiar" in that very same Bible. African Americans are "a peculiar people."

The word peculiar in the Biblical context means; *"one's very own, special, purchased possession, and/or property."* Yes, God described the Hebrews in this manner. Embrace your peculiarity! In many instances, this additional information added missing pieces to a puzzle. With God-given discernment, I have encountered brow-raising details on some pages of these books. However, I have been far more enlightened and am thankful for a greater understanding of who I am – why I am here and my rightful place in God's kingdom. In conclusion, one of the directives adopted by those who believed these books should be part of the Bible in the early church was to read them as life instructional reads, not Doctrine. This perspective is appropriate. One thing to keep in mind is they bring clarity and add the missing information. The Doctrine of Christ is established. The place of the original Hebrews requires further reading and understanding, and these ancient writings help in that regard. In today's society, books related to the historical truths of slavery and African American history are being removed from classrooms and libraries. The generations to come will discover them and add what is missing or kept secret. Let's be clear. Hidden does not mean without truth. It is often the truth that is hidden to protect one's personal agenda, crime, or a person's feelings.

Hidden Books Rich History

We have established a brief history of the Apocrypha. Now let's explore five interesting books: Jubilees, Baruch, Enoch, and 1st and 2nd Maccabees, three of which are not part of the Christian Canon nor the Apocrypha and two that are part of the Apocrypha but not the Christian Canon of Scriptures.

While these books did not make the cut for inclusion, they are a part of the canonized Ethiopian Bible and provide invaluable insight into missing history and understanding of the canonized version of the Christian Bible.

It is your decision to study them, but it is highly recommended that you do. If nothing else, read them as Christian novels – but read them! Hosea 4:6(a) reads:

"My people are destroyed for lack of knowledge..." (ESV).

Living in ignorance is living in perpetual bondage. Sure, the physical shackles and chains have been broken, but the spiritual and mental ones remain. The Bible says true worshippers' *"worship in spirit and in truth."* It is time to break free.

The Books of Baruch and the Maccabees are part of the Christian Apocrypha and are highly recommended. However, The Books of Maccabees are challenging to read mainly because the storyline is entirely new to some students of the Bible. In addition, some of the common names attached to familiar biblical figures refer to completely different people. I have included brief narratives on each of these hidden or secret books. Regarding the caution I received about not using these books as outside sources, I concluded from my experience that the warnings were baseless and probably unexplored by those who cautioned me against them. I thought I would find blasphemous or insidious information in them that would condemn me.

What I found were some questionable events, meaning they seemed far-fetched in the grand scheme of the Bible, or stories with missing links to known Doctrine. Nevertheless, their overall information is invaluable – historical content – directly related to the original Hebrew people.

I also discovered – what I thought I knew of the Bible was less than I actually did. 1st and 2nd Maccabees helped me to better understand more of the historical context of the New Testament.

Once I began to grasp this knowledge, I sought understanding. I began to see the Bible in living color. For example, the book titled *"Hebrews"* in the Bible – brought so much clarity upon discovering the original title, *"To the Hebrew People."* I will forever refer to the original name from now on. The name itself brings on a completely different perspective. It no longer fits into a witty joke about coffee. Get it, He – Brews. It is about God's chosen people. It now makes total sense to me. What seemed to be disjointed, disconnected, and mysterious is now a cohesive understanding.

Repeat out loud the word **Hebrews**. Then repeat out loud "**To the Hebrew People**." There is a big difference! This is a minor wordsmithing that leads to a major difference in understanding.

When I read the Bible now, I see "myself," I see my people (African Americans), and our dilemma, but more importantly, I understand why we are in the space and place of time that we are. I am awake! I get it! Please join me on this underground ride to freedom. Harriett Tubman said she could have freed more slaves if they only knew they were slaves. The same principle applies to the truth of our plight today. Get on board.

Book of Jasher

The Book of Jasher is referenced in the Bible in 2 Samuel 1:18 and Joshua 10:13 ...

"Is it not written in the Book of Jasher?" (NIV)

Jasher's name means Righteous or Upright. The Book of Jasher was originally translated as *"The Book of the Upright or the Book of the Just Man."* The manuscript of this book was found in a cave in 1947 in a remote Judean desert along with hundreds of other ancient documents written on scrolls known as The Dead Sea Scrolls. Jasher covers the history of the world from creation until the period of the Judges in Israel (Pratt, 2020).

The Book of Jasher provides more insight into the genealogy of Japheth, Shem and Ham. This is extremely important when putting together those missing pieces of the puzzle that have the African American dissociated from the rest of humanity. It also highlights the superpowers that the Hebrews possessed, much like in the movie, "Black Panther."

An example from The Book of Jasher providing more historical context is as follows:

"And Cain hastened and rose up, and took the iron part of his plowing instrument, with which he suddenly smote his brother and he slew him and Cain spilled the blood of his brother Abel upon the earth, and the blood of Abel streamed upon the earth before the flock. And after this Cain repented having slain his brother, and he was sadly grieved, and he wept over him, and it vexed him exceedingly" (Jasher 1:25-26).

As we read further down, verse *1:29[b]* reads:

"And the Lord said unto him, 'What has thou done? The voice of thy brother's blood crieth unto me from the ground where thou has slain him'."

From this account, we learn how Cain killed Abel with a more retrospective understanding of Abel's blood being spilled upon the ground, along with God's response to it.

The account in Genesis says:

"Now Cain said to his brother Abel, Let's go out to the field. And while they were in the field, Cain attacked his brother Abel and killed him" (Genesis 4:8 NIV).

Then in verse 10, we read:

"The Lord said, What have you done? Listen! Your brother's blood cries out to me from the ground" (NIV).

The natural inclination from the Genesis account would be to believe that something in "the attack" caused Abel to bleed, whereas the Book of Jasher takes away the contemplative thought and gives the detail. Detail makes a difference. *"The blood of Abel streams upon the earth before the flock!"*

That statement parallels the blood of Jesus Christ flowing before His flock in the New Testament of the Bible. It was the blood of Jesus Christ that saved humanity! It was His blood poured out on Calvary that brought us reconciliation with God and eternal life. His shed blood from an act of violence by haters brought forgiveness of sins, redemption, healing, and miracles.

There is power in the blood of Jesus. Yet, the blood of the Hebrews scattered abroad cries out from the ground!

Jasher also clarifies the narrative of Lot's wife in the Christian Bible and provides her name.

"And he overthrew these cities, all the plain and all the inhabitants of the cities, and that which grew upon the ground; and 'Ado, the wife of Lot looked back to see the destruction of the cities, for her compassion, was moved on account of her daughters who remained in Sodom, for they did not go with her" (Jasher 19:52).

The account in Genesis in the canonized Bible does not give the possible reason she looked back nor provide her name. We are not informed that "all" of Lot's daughters did not leave Sodom. My understanding of why Lot's wife (Ado) defied God and looked back was because she longed for the "good" life they were leaving behind! Is that the correct interpretation of the story? Well, yes, if that is the only part of the story recorded. Certainly, one could argue the key point of obedience. She was told not to look back, and she did. The rest is history. It doesn't matter! Or does it?

This account in Jasher brings a more clarifying and feministic view. As a woman, a mother, how would that bring different enlightenment?

A mother's love is sacrificial. A mother's love for her child is unconditional. A mother's love will take certain risks. A mother's love is unbreakable. A mother's love would find it difficult to leave a child in danger. A mother's love can be irrational, as it comes from the deep recesses of the soul, in the same way, the Father (God) sought to protect her.

I am not justifying her action, just highlighting that the interpretation I have been accustomed to may not be accurate given additional detail.

This book is filled with rich history, including more information on Enoch, Noah, Abraham, Moses, Nimrod, Esau, and their lineage. It provides names of several other women as well who are not specifically named in the Canonized version of the Bible.

Additionally, it lets us know that Noah and Abraham lived during one another's times. They knew each other. Jasher tells us what happened to the clothing of animal skins that God made for Adam when he was escorted out of the Garden of Eden and the power within the garments.

It provides a prophecy of Abram(ham)'s greatness and how he had to live hidden in a cave for ten years to save his life. The text reads as follows:

> *"And when Abram came out from the cave, he went to Noah and his son Shem, and he remained with them to learn the instruction of the Lord and his ways, and no man knew where Abram(ham) was, and Abram(ham) served Noah and Shem his son for a long time" (Jasher 9:5).*

Jasher tells of God's love for Abram(ham) and his hand of protection over him in Jasher 37:14:

The Book records several prayers:

> *"And Jacob prayed to the Lord for his sons and he spread forth his hands to the Lord, and he said, O God,*

thou art an Almighty God, thou art our Father, thou didst form us and we are works of thine hands; I pray thee deliver my sons through thy mercy from the hands of their enemies, who are this day coming to fight with them, and save them from their hand, for in thy hand, is power and might, to save the few from the many."

This is an on-time prayer that would be beneficial to pray over our children every day.

If you want to connect dots that are missing in Scripture, this is a good resource to do so. It fills in a lot of blank spaces. It is a recommended read for deeper understanding and clarity.

We know it existed because the canonized version of the Bible mentions it more than once.

Book of Jubilees

The name or title Jubilees means "Ram's Horn.". The Book of Jubilees recounts events in forty-nine-year spans (seven cycles of seven) as described in the Book of Leviticus. The beginning of every Jubilee was recognized by the sound of the Ram's horn.

The Book of Jubilees was part of a discovery of manuscripts found in the Dead Sea Scrolls. It dates to the first century A.D.

Though it was not canonized, it does provide historical content not found in the canonized Christian Bible. For example, it gives detail on the Nephilim[1], providing a more comprehensive understanding of their works. As mentioned earlier, it pinpoints the exact location of the Garden of Eden.

Jubilees is stated to have some discrepancies when studied against the Bible. However, it does add some valuable information and provides some clarity to help connect the dots of missing information.

---

1 Nephilim- Giants

We learn more about Abram(ham)'s calling from birth into his service to God. According to Jubilees, God blessed Abram(ham) after he prayed and asked God to deliver him and his family from the "evil spirits" that had consumed the earth and man. God then told him to move, and that is when he journeyed to Canaan and Egypt. This account is not found in the Christian Bible. It is titled; *"The Call of Abraham"* in the Book of Jubilees.

The backdrop of the prayer comes from a discussion Abram(ham) had with his father regarding his father's idolatry. We know that Abram(ham) was a righteous man, but we learn of the depth of his piety in this non-canonized book.

The Book of Jubilees also gives a clear account of Canaan (Ham's descendants) illegally taking the land given to Shem's descendants. This is important in understanding how Canaan obtained what was given to Shem's descendants. They just took it – and that is still happening to the descendants of Shem to this day. Resources, wealth, cities bombed, businesses destroyed, gentrification, communities destroyed, highways built through neighborhoods are still in full effect – possessions just taken and re-occupied.

Book of Baruch

A significant opening to the Book of Baruch[2] states: *"A Message to a Conquered People."* The title alone caught my attention!

Baruch is part of the Apocrypha and was included in the original canonized version of the Christian Bible but later removed.

Baruch mentions more than once, *"The people of Israel **and** Judah,"* which distinguishes them from the other tribes. They were divided, but both were wicked and sinned in historical accounts.

2 Scripture references for the Book of Baruch are taken from The Revised English Bible with The Apocrypha (1995). Oxford University Press and Cambridge University Press.

There are disputes regarding the dates or time frame of this book's writing, but it speaks to similar experiences relative to African Americans. It is an interesting read – short and focused.

There is a confession, prayer for deliverance, and memory of God's promises to His people. The confessions, prayers, and cries for wisdom are relevant to African Americans today.

"Why is it, Israel, that you are in your enemies' country, grown old in a foreign land" (Baruch 3:10 REB)?

Why is it African Americans – you are in a foreign land?

"Take heart, my people, who keep Israel's name alive. You were sold to the heathen, but not to be destroyed. Because you excited God's wrath you were handed over to the foe, for you provoked your Maker by sacrificing not to God but to demons. You forgot the eternal God who nurtured you; you caused sorrow to Jerusalem who fostered you" (Baruch 4:5-8 REB).

Repent!

"Come you neighbors of Zion, bear in mind the captivity of my sons and daughters inflicted on them by the Eternal; for he let loose on them a nation from afar, a ruthless nation speaking a strange tongue and with no reverence for the old, no pity for the young. They carried off the widow's beloved sons, and left her in loneliness, bereft of her daughters. But how can I help you? Only the One who brought the disasters on you can deliver you from the power of your enemies" (Baruch 4:14-18 REB).

Let that sink in!

"They went away from you on foot, led off by their enemies; but God is bringing them home to you, borne aloft in glory, as on a royal throne" (Baruch 5:6 REB).

God never leaves his people without hope. The *Book of Baruch* is short, easy-to-read and recommended.

Enoch

The word "secret" is, in part, the definition of the word Apocrypha. Enoch would fit in that category from my perspective.

Enoch is said to be the first written Book of the Bible; even before Moses. It was initially part of the Canon but was removed years later. However, Enoch is part of the Ethiopian Bible.

Enoch is referenced in the canonized Christian Bible in the Book of Jude. Jude uses a quote from 1 Enoch, testifying to the truth of Enoch's prophecy. It reads:

> *"It was also about these that Enoch, the seventh from Adam, prophesied, saying, Behold, the Lord comes with ten thousands of his holy ones..." (Jude 1:4 ESV).*

Enoch provides a more in-depth teaching of the fallen angels, demonic activity on earth, and the actual creation.

Enoch speaks a lot about judgment for specific sins and those who committed those sins.

Enoch gives an in-depth insight into the functions of the sun, moon, earth, stars, and orbits.

Enoch provides details no other books give, including the dynamics of the universe.

Here are some interesting facts about Enoch:

He is documented to be the first man able to read and write.

Enoch was taken up to heaven alive.

Enoch walked with God, indicating he had a close relationship with Him.

Enoch was born in sin but lived a godly life.

Enoch was alive during Noah's days, which at that time, were some of the most wicked times on the face of the earth. The world is not far off.

Regarding his writings, Enoch says:

> *"And now, my son Methuselah, all these things I am recounting to you and writing down for you. And I have revealed to you everything, and given you books concerning all these; so, my son Methuselah, preserve the books from your father's hand, and see that you deliver them to the generations of the world. I have given wisdom to you and to your children, and those children to come, that they may give it to their children for generations. This wisdom namely that passes their understanding. And those who understand it shall not sleep, but shall listen that they may learn this wisdom, and it shall please those that eat thereof better than food" (Enoch 82:1-3).*[3]

Wake up. This book is heavy – but is a recommended read.

Books of Maccabees

The Books of Maccabees are also "highly recommended reads." The events recorded in the Maccabees books occurred between the Old and New Testaments. They are not a quick and easy read, but if you want to dig deep into understanding the New Testament – you will want to read these books. Maccabees I & II are included in the Apocrypha. These books are also housed within their own book which contains 4 or 5 books depending on the source.

---

3 Lumpkin, J. (2011) The Books of Enoch.

Let's peek at some interesting scriptures from this book.

> "...Her infants are slain in her streets, her young
> men by the sword of the foe. Is there any nation
> that has not usurped her sovereignty, any people
> that has not taken plunder from her? She has been
> stripped of all her adornment; she is no longer
> free; she is a slave" (1 Maccabees 2:9-11 REB).

I wrote in the margin of my Bible the word "Wow" by this text and encircled it. If this is not specific to African Americans, it certainly gives a chilling resemblance to their known history.

Given that – what can we learn from it? What can we pull from it to rise above our current standard of living? The Bible and hidden Biblical sources encompass the self-help books we need. Now, let's look at a recorded prayer;

> "Lord God, the Creator of all things, the terrible and
> mighty, the just and merciful, the only King, you alone
> are gracious; you are the only Giver, the only just and
> omnipotent and eternal One, the Deliverer of Israel
> from every evil, who chose the patriarchs and set
> them apart. Accept we pray, this sacrifice on behalf
> of your whole people Israel; watch over them and
> sanctify them, for they are your own possession. Bring
> together those of our people who are dispersed, set
> free those who are enslaved among the heathen, look
> favorably on those who are despised and detested;
> so, let the heathen know that you are our God. Punish
> with torments our arrogant and insolent oppressors,
> and as promised by Moses, plant your people in
> your holy land" (2 Maccabees 1:24-29 REB).

The Maccabees fought for Jewish independence against the political structure and rulers of the time with great passion.

These books are rich with history that is virgin to many of our learnings.

REFLECTIONS

_____

_____

_____

_____

_____

_____

_____

_____

_____

_____

_____

_____

_____

_____

_____

_____

_____

_____

_____

_____

_____

_____

_____

CHAPTER SEVEN

TOWER OF BABEL
SCATTERED— NOT LOST!
GENESIS 11

T he Tower of Babel! That sounds like it could be a mystery, thriller, horror movie. Well, that is close to how God viewed it. This small story in the Bible greatly impacted how the areas of the earth were populated following the Flood. God instructed Noah's sons to voluntarily scatter themselves across the earth on three separate occasions. There was just one language at the time, which they all spoke. Instead of doing as instructed, under the direction of one of Noah's grandsons (Nimrod), they rebelled. They picked out some prime property, camped out, and began passionately building a city and tower for themselves that would reach the Heavens. The structure was massive. They spent 45 years building it, and it took one full year to climb to the top of the tower. It was no small notion. Their intent against God was vile, as you will see in the text. God will allow foolishness for just so long before he shows up and shows out.

God's answer resulted in the second great judgment upon the earth. As part of His judgment, God confused their language and scattered them abroad — the very thing they were trying to avoid. Like foreigners from different lands, they could talk but not decipher what the next person was saying. This resulted in the sound of babble.

Have you ever wondered where certain sayings began? Sometimes we accuse others of babbling when we do not understand the language they are communicating. When a person or a baby babbles, they make sounds that are not understood. This language is called babble. The origin of the word babble could be rooted in this story of the Bible.

As for God's judgment, we read:

> "So, the Lord dispersed them from there over the face of all the earth, and they left off building the city. Therefore, its name was called Babel, because there the Lord confused the language of all the earth. And from there the Lord dispersed them over the face of all the earth" (Genesis 11:8-9 ESV).[1]

Let's review the account of this from The Book of Jasher. It gives more detail than the canonized account of the Bible.

> "And the building of the tower was unto them a transgression and a sin, and they began to build it, and whilst they were building against the Lord God of heaven, they imagined in their hearts to war against him and to ascend into heaven. And all these people [you people]* and all the families divided themselves in three parts; the first said We will ascend into heaven and fight against him; the second said, We will ascend to heaven and place our own gods there and serve them; and the third part said We will ascend to heaven and smite him with bows and spears; and God knew all their works and all their evil thoughts and he saw the city and the tower which they were building" (Jasher 9:25-26).

---

1 There are between 1500 and 2000 languages spoken in Africa!

*Emphasis authors!

> "And the Lord smote the three divisions that were
> there, and he punished them according to their works
> and designs; those who said We will ascend to heaven
> and serve our gods, <u>became like apes</u> <u>and</u> <u>elephants</u>;[2]
> and those who said, We will smite the heaven with
> arrows, the Lord killed them, one man through the
> hand of his neighbor; and the third division of those
> who said, We will ascend to heaven and fight him,
> the Lord scattered throughout the earth." And those
> who were left amongst them, when they knew and
> understood the evil which was coming upon them, they
> forsook the building, and they also became scattered
> upon the face of the whole earth (Jasher 9:35-36).

> "And when the Lord had scattered the sons of men
> on account of their sin at the Tower, behold they
> spread forth into many divisions, and all the sons
> of men were dispersed into the four corners of the
> earth. And all the families became each according to
> its language, its land, or its city" (Jasher 10:2-3).

The significance of this study is that the Tribes of Israel were scattered across the face of the earth. Scattered because of rebellious spirits, arrogance, disobedience, and pride. Nevertheless, that is how nations and races landed where they are today.

Now that we can travel the world from the comfort of our digital devices, and as more of the truth is revealed, we can see that Negroes are indeed "everywhere." Yes, even to the uttermost parts of the earth. The planted seed in African Americans is that dark-skinned people were enslaved from Africa. That's it. They are from the jungles of Africa with no known connections.

---

2 No clarity is given on this comment, but it could explain where the stigma on Black men came from.

Many African Americans are just discovering the vast dispersion of their ancestors was not just to America. Technology has allowed all to see different regions of the world and different peoples of the world that have a striking resemblance to African Americans, especially in Africa and areas of the Islands. The trusted historian Josephus states:

> *"There were some also who passed over the*
> *sea in ships and inhabited the islands...".*

Have you ever stopped to consider how it is that African Americans resemble people of color all around the world? "Dark-skinned people" in Jamaica and Haiti have been known, but a connection to African Americans on other Islands was treated as a mystery. Wow – where did they come from? They talk with different accents. They speak different languages – who are they, and how did they get there?

When traveling, there are times the identity of African Americans would not be detected based on appearance. It is given away by their diction! God did not create African Americans different from other dark-skinned people around the world. He scattered them across the globe.

The love of the universal language of music has further opened this window as artists travel and are welcomed abroad and in America and discover the dispersion.

Think about a sheet of paper torn into pieces. Then imagine throwing those pieces of paper up into the wind and watching them scatter. In time, some of those pieces will become more and more distant. The missing pieces will remain obscure as other pieces are retrieved and placed back together. However, you know that pieces were detached – they existed and were scattered in the wind – but you have no idea where they were scattered. The larger piece of paper will never be complete until those scattered pieces are retrieved and placed back into the whole. That is where African Americans find themselves -

scattered – separated from the whole. Scattered, as the Bible says – across the four corners of the earth.

Reflecting back to the definition of the Pishon River, it symbolizes the dispersion of the Israelites. The Hebrew word means; shaking the region; great diffusion, break apart or scatter; tear in pieces. Symbolically that is what occurred to the Hebrew people.

There is a scripture in 2 Chronicles 7:14 that we love to quote in times of trouble. It is directly prophetic of the plight of a peculiar people in this life.

> *"If my people who are called by my name humble themselves and pray and seek my face and turn from their wicked ways, then I will hear from heaven and will forgive their sin and heal their land" (ESV).*

This is a community call to repentance among a group of peculiar people. But until we fully grasp and understand the gravity of this charge, our current condition will remain. African Americans will continue to be appalled at other people and other people will continue to be appalled at them. The vicious cycle will continue.

It was following this event at the Tower of Babel that God chose the Hebrews as his own.

REFLECTIONS

CHAPTER EIGHT

Sins of the Hebrews

The Hebrews – God's beloved and chosen people-sinned against Him repeatedly with their idolatry! God made it very clear where He stands on idolatry.

"I am the Lord your God, who brought you out of Egypt, out of the land of slavery. You shall have no other gods before me. You shall not make for yourself an idol in the form of anything in Heaven above or on the earth beneath, or in the waters below" (Exodus 20:2-4 BSB).[1]

What is idolatry? According to *Zondervan's Bible Dictionary,* *"idolatry in ancient times included two forms of departure from the true religion: the worship of false gods, whether with images or otherwise; and the worship of the Lord utilizing images (Douglas & Tenney, 1987)."* Idolatry involves anything you worship to the extent of being consumed in and with that item. For example, money can be an idol, shoes, a job, or your significant other. On a smaller scale, we do not often think about the items mentioned above being idols to us, but depending on our relationship to the item, they are. The Hebrews had many idols or 'gods' that they

---

1 Berean Standard Bible (2021). Online. https://biblegateway.com/versions

worshipped instead of the true and living God. They brought their idols with them out of Egypt and had become comfortable in the Egyptians' culture, and way of life. This sin was part of their DNA, and if we are honest about it – it is still part of our DNA. Therefore, it is so important that we not only recognize and acknowledge our sins but that we must turn from them.

Before I came into the knowledge of who I am, not only in Christ but in God's chosen people, I would read about the Hebrew people and become disgusted with them – extremely judgmental. Now that I am enlightened to the truth, I want to share this information that we are not taught or aware of because the disgust in them is now - me. I am them. You are them. We **are** those [people]!

Only a Hebrew could get on God's nerves as they did. You will see what I mean as you read through the following examples! We tend to focus on the promises in the Prophetic Books of Isaiah, Jeremiah, and Ezekiel and avoid the warnings. We avoid the Book of Lamentations completely, except for a verse or two that is pleasant to our hearing! Is the avoidance because we do not understand it? Perhaps it is because we do not believe it pertains to us? Think again!

There are stark warnings and teachings in the Prophetic Books of the Bible. Unlocking the history of the Hebrews is the key to correcting said behaviors moving forward.

Think about it – African Americans, in general, cannot even trace their known heritage past the slave ship. Some cannot even trace that far. Certainly, this has changed with the use of tools like Ancestry.com and similar services; but not everyone can contract these services or have the knowledge and resources to do so. I might add even more alarming – a disinterest in wanting to learn.

When I went to get vaccinated for my first trip to Africa, the nurse administering my shot asked me what I wanted to go to

Africa for in an irritated tone. I sarcastically replied, to see your cousins! She, in turn, was offended as though I had slapped her in the face and quickly retorted:

"My people are from Louisiana.
I have no connection to them."

While in Africa, I was at a school, and the School Master resembled this nurse. I told her that someone in America looked very much like her and asked if it were okay to take her picture. She smiled – beamed, actually and said yes. When I returned to the doctor's office following my trip, I showed the picture of the African woman to the nurse and said I found one of your cousins. She looked at the picture and was literally speechless. Even she could not deny the striking resemblance. When the doctor came in to see me, I shared the picture and story with her, and she was simply amazed by the resemblance. She asked how her nurse responded and I told her after I pushed her to respond, she simply stuck to her story; her people are from Louisiana! No, my sister, that is where your slave master is from!

We have accepted being despised by society and participating in despising and denying our own. We can do that when we do not have a known identity to anyone. We can become attached to whomever we choose, reasoning they are who they are, but I have no connection to them. This is a sentiment that allows us to mentally disassociate ourselves. Nevertheless, over time we get fed up with repeated injustices. To express our frustrations, we utilize the right to protest. Over the years, some protests have been peaceful demonstrations and others have not. We have learned that protests are easily accessible, draw temporary attention, and give us an allusion to being heard. It allows us to express anger if the setting remains controlled per the oppressor's comfort level.

What happens after the dust settles? We settle back into our routines – until the next egregious act against us, individually or collectively, occurs. We go back to living without closure, clarity, or understanding. We blow off a little steam until the heat is turned down. We then go back to the familiar because even in the most violent storms, once it is over, a calmness follows. That is nature, and the same principle applies to our lives. Consequently, we become anesthetized to the pain during the calm period and take the breather while we can.

Even through our sins, God has a plan in place to bring us back to Himself with full redemption. Just like He delivered Daniel from the lion's den and the Israelites from the Egyptians. He is going to deliver us. But we must trust in His Word and His sovereignty. Let's explore some scriptures from the Bible that will resonate now that you know the truth.

> *"Now therefore say to the people of Judah and those living in Jerusalem, 'This is what the Lord says: Look! I am preparing a disaster for you and devising a plan against you. So, turn from your evil ways, each one of you, and reform your ways and your actions. But they will reply, 'It's no use. We will continue with our own plans; each of us will follow the stubbornness of his evil heart. Therefore, this is what the Lord says: Inquire among the nations: Who has ever heard anything like this? A most horrible thing has been done by Virgin Israel. Does the snow of Lebanon ever vanish from its rocky slopes? Do its cool waters from distant sources ever cease to flow? Yet my people have forgotten me; they burn incense to worthless idols, which made them stumble in their ways and in the ancient paths. They made them walk in bypaths and on roads not built up. Their land will be laid waste, an object of lasting scorn; **all who pass by will be appalled and will shake their heads. Like the wind from the east, I will scatter them before their enemies;** I will show them my back and not my face in the day of their disaster" (Jeremiah 18:11-17 NIV).*

Think about that. In our major cities in America and elsewhere, we have been scattered among our enemies; people, do in fact, "drive by" and shake their heads at the conditions of black people. We are appalled that they are appalled – and neither one of us knows why it is appalling.

Throughout several other books of the Bible: Judges, Kings, and Chronicles, for example, we see a constant battle with the desire to serve idols. People would build images and worship the image in abundance. Then God would raise a leader to tear them down and warn them. God will raise some devout men and women who will lead us according to His instructions. The Bible states false prophets will rise. Therefore, it is critical to know the Word to discern that whoever rises as our next leader is sent from God. We have already followed false prophecies and accepted carefully constructed mistruths.

Because we have built these altars again, we constantly battle between good and evil. What feels good, does not always mean good. What is our motto today, "if it feels good—do it." Or how about "Just Do It." Listen, Hebrews, we cannot "Just Do It" without consequences. They forgot to give us the fine print!

For practical purposes, let's look at the Biblical examples found in the characters of the false gods Baal and his counterparts Ashtoreth and Asherah. The Hebrews worshipped and followed some of the practices of these "gods" introduced to them by the early Egyptians as they intermixed.

Baal was worshipped as a supreme god and was also a false prophet. Under his religious rites, child sacrifices were practiced, in which children were placed and burned on an altar alive; divination and prostitution were common.

Fast forward – today, we follow false prophets, abandon our children, and sacrifice them to television, social media, and material goods while looking to fortune-tellers to predict our future. We sacrifice them to stray bullets that we spread, shooting at one another while speeding through residential streets where our innocent children are outside playing, or even, in some cases, at home, sleeping.

Ashtoreth was worshipped as a fertility goddess very similar to Asherah and linked to Baal. As such, we will focus our discussion on Asherah. Ashtoreth is mentioned in 1 Samuel 7.

Asherah (also known as Astarte) was worshipped as the supreme goddess of fertility and was believed to be the giver of life. We have then an inanimate idol being worshipped instead of the Creator, Sustainer, and true Giver of life. Asherah was also a goddess of pleasure - a sex goddess. She was linked to music, sexual dances, and alcohol. Basically, she was the goddess of "freak offs."

She was worshipped through carved images made of wood, known as Asherah Poles. These poles were widespread, placed on high hills and common throughout the land, including in the Temple of God.

She was sometimes depicted with enlarged breasts, cupping them with her hands. Other images show her half-naked standing on the back of a lion. There are images showing her with a snake wrapped around a wooden pole.

Today, we are hooked on pornography and have constant battles to free ourselves from it. Our girls and young women prostitute themselves in music videos. Some of our churches today resemble the Temple and consequently are not free from her spirit.

Perhaps that is why thousands of years later, men still view women as sex objects, and pole dancing is such a lucrative business. We have not gotten rid of that spirit from among us.

You can find scriptures in the Books of Deuteronomy, 1 and 2 Kings, 1 and 2 Chronicles, and Judges as well as a reference in the New Testament to these inanimate idols worshipped as living gods. This is one of the egregious forms of idolatry we replaced the true worship of a Living God with.

Throughout the Old Testament, breaking free from worshipping these inanimate idols was a constant battle. The Bible gives us God's extreme displeasure of them - an abomination and detestable.

I remember several years ago in Detroit (and I am not isolating Detroit), a fifteen-year-old girl was dancing at a very popular topless bar. The bar was cited and padlocked for allowing a minor to perform. A few months later, this same *child* was busted dancing again at another club in the city. That spirit is so strong and disregards so blatant for this *child* that she was sacrificed for the pleasure of others, more specifically - grown men.

Then, of course, we have the famous worship of golden images. A golden image was an image built out of gold and worshipped. Today, it's bling, and we have advanced from gold to platinum.

There was also Min, the god of fertility. To show his role as the god of male potency, he depicted himself with an erect penis (which appears to be enlarged). You can view this by searching for Ancient Egyptian gods in books or on the Internet. Today some of our men and younger men are fixated with their perception of sexual potency.

What is the significance of this dialogue? To help us understand the depths of the sinful historical and sexual behaviors, along with the impact it has had on the community. An impact that is unhealthy and debilitating. The momentary pleasure it brings results in the deaths of marriages, families, communities, and growth as a people.

To put it bluntly, it is keeping African Americans as a community from God. God views African Americans (Hebrews) as a community – a people unto Himself. Society views African Americans as a cohesive community. Unfortunately, African Americans are the ones who separate themselves from one another. Now, this is not to say it is all-inclusive, because God keeps a remnant of pious people; however, it is a community problem that stems from historical behaviors.

In Leviticus 18:24-25, God gives the Israelites this warning:

"Do not make yourselves unclean by any of these things. For by all these the nations I am driving out before you have become unclean, and the land became unclean so that I punished its iniquity, and the land vomited out its inhabitants" (ESV).

Imagine just for a moment what the earth would look like if it were to vomit itself. I recall the 2006 Tsunami in Asia as an example of what that could look like. A Tsunami is an earthquake from the depths of the ocean. At that time, I wasn't even aware of what a tsunami was. That tsunami brought forth waves that reached 60 feet high and left a trail of death, debris, destruction, and disease in the land.

Vomit: To eject the contents of the stomach through the mouth; regurgitate; throw up; to belch or spew with force or violence; to eject from the stomach through the mouth; spew; to cast out or eject as if in vomiting; send out forcefully or violently. (Random House Kernerman Webster's College Dictionary, 2010).

That definition is not pleasant, nor is the act of vomiting, yet it is how God described his displeasure. It was not intended to be pretty. Physically though, once a person vomits, they are ready to be healed because the toxin has been expelled.

For the Hebrew people to be healed as a community, we must study our Biblical history. Not just American History or the little we know of it because that is just a tangible affect of our oppressed lives. We need to know beyond a certainty of a doubt who we are and who we were created to be in God. We need to get to the root of the problem. We need to know and understand that our history did not begin when that first slave ship landed in Jamestown, Virginia.

African American history begins in the Garden of Eden with their ancestral parents, Adam, and Eve, just like every other nation (race) in this world.

How in the world have we accepted the planted and well-watered seed, that we just happened upon the earth, a broken, sinful, useless group of people suitable only for a Tarzan movie? Even though we are living in the land of the free and the home of the brave, it is those subliminal and implanted images and practices that keep us in bondage.

It is my belief that until we (African Americans) develop true knowledge of our ancestors in our homeland and connect in joint sufferings, our situations will not greatly change. African Americans' suffering is tied to the suffering of our people because we are a community of people.

Society has the self-righteous, prideful audacity to pity the condition of children in other countries. These children can be seen in commercials, living in extreme poverty, with dirty skin and blank stares, as though we can see clearly through a projected image of empty souls. It draws pity. In the words of Daffy Duck, those broadcasts are despicable! Not that extreme poverty does not exist, but the exploitation of the circumstances is unconscionable. Did you ever stop to think about the similarity to America's youth – even though the United States of America is the richest country in the world? Do you not see abandonment, hunger, despair, death, helplessness, and homelessness in some of the youth right here in America? We must remove the plank from our eyes. What is the difference? In America, we tend to believe the carrot we see dangling in front of us, which gives us an allusion of riches at hand's reach, that we have arrived. We have the same problems, played out on a different note.

We talked about the Tower of Babel earlier and how God scattered the Hebrews. A huge part of that story goes even deeper than just the foolishness of their actions and intentions. The structure they were building was phenomenal. It was so advanced, and their efforts so intense God "came down" to see what they were doing. They were brilliant. They were powerful. The problem is they were planning to take over God's domain. We have some amazingly brilliant minds. We still use our brilliance inappropriately. We do not find too many African Americans coming up on the "Dumbest Criminals" stories list!

Society still tries to keep African Americans confused and separated for that same reason, with the exception it is not for our good, but because of their fear. In the workplace, if more than two African Americans are having lunch or just off having a conversation, it gets interrupted!

There are many references to the sins of the Israelites and Hebrews in scripture. We find another convicting warning in Jeremiah 29:18-19 which reads:

> *"I will pursue them with the sword, famine, and plague*
> *and will make them abhorrent to all the kingdoms*
> *of the earth, a curse, and an object of horror, of*
> *scorn and reproach, among all the nations where I drive*
> *them. For they have not listened to my words," declares*
> *the Lord, "words that I sent to them again and*
> *again by my servants the prophets. And you exiles*
> *have not listened either," declares the Lord" (NIV).*

Finally, for consideration, but certainly not the least or last, we read in Jeremiah 17:4-5:

> *"You shall loosen your hand from your heritage that I*
> *gave to you, and I will make you serve your enemies in*
> *a land that you do not know, for in my anger a fire is*
> *kindled that shall burn forever. Thus says the Lord.*

*Cursed is the man who trusts in man and
makes flesh his strength, whose heart
turns away from the Lord" (ESV).*

Is there any other nation on earth that fits this category as described? It is the opinion of the author that there is not. When we look at the corners of every major city in America and in Black-dominated countries around the world, this is a recurring theme; we are an object of horror, scorn, and reproach.

The problem, before this information, rested on our not knowing or understanding why. Why are African Americans despised everywhere we tread? Why are African Americans unable to stick together as a nation? African Americans are now without excuse. God is removing the covering from our eyes so that we can see. *"Let he who has ears hear what the Spirit is saying..."*

The Hebrews lost favor with God because of their sins and disobedience. Even with that, they are God's chosen people. Salvation is available to everyone – but the promises of the land in Jerusalem are available only to the Hebrew people. As you think about it, understand the land (Israel) was taken – and it will one day be returned to its rightful owners.

African Americans have not had the benefit of living on their own land since they were exiled over 400 years ago. We are reminded daily the soil on which we live does not belong to us. After 400 years, we are still aliens in the land our ancestors cultivated and built. We may have made some minor gains, to which some eventually got removed, or we may find ourselves uprooted.

Stories like the 1921 Tulsa, Oklahoma massacre, the incident in Rosewood, California, or the deliberate installation of freeways through neighborhoods that destroyed vibrant communities are never-ending. I lived in one of those areas where a freeway was cut right through the center of a neighborhood – uprooting hundreds of families and downgrading the standard of living. It was the beginning of the ultimate demise of a nice working-class neighborhood. Neighbors knew one another. Kids played outside together and ate dinner at one another's homes. Cups of sugar, flour, milk, an egg, or two were freely exchanged among neighbors instead of having to run to the store. The sense of community was destroyed! As the original residents left and the neighborhood transitioned, drugs were brought in, delivering the final blow to the neighborhood.

The Book of Lamentations gives some valuable insight into the problem, beginning with the opening Chapter, Lamentations 1:1, which reads:

"How deserted lies the city, once so full of people! How like a widow is she who once was great among the nations! She who was queen among the provinces has now become a slave." We read further in Lamentations 1:3; "After affliction and harsh labor, Judah has gone into exile. She dwells among the nations; she finds no resting place. All who pursue her have overtaken her in the midst of her distress" (NIV).

Lamentations 2:11:

"My eyes fail from weeping. I am in torment within, my heart is poured out on the ground because my people are destroyed because children and infants faint in the streets of the city" (NIV).

Lamentations 2:19:

"Arise, cry out in the night, as the watches of the night begin; pour out your heart like water in the presence of the Lord. Lift up your hands to him for the lives of your children, who faint from hunger at the head of every street" (NIV).

God still shows compassion and gives hope amid disaster in His faithfulness to the covenantal promises. Lamentations 3:22:

> *Because of the Lord's great love we are not consumed, for his compassions never fail. They are new every morning; great is your faithfulness" (NIV).*

God is faithful even when we are not faithful to Him. He continues to give us new mercies every day. What do you do with them?

REFLECTIONS

CHAPTER NINE

PROMISES TO THE HEBREW PEOPLE

W e took a snapshot of some scriptures regarding the sins of the Hebrews. Now let us balance that with some promises. As stated previously, we should note; while God grafted the Gentiles (non-Jewish people) into salvation, there are specific promises that pertain only to His chosen people, the Hebrews. The often quoted and very familiar passage of scripture below provides not only the Hebrew people's relevance to God but also what blessings those who are good to His people will receive. This was the promise God made to Abram(ham) when He called him into His service. We read in Genesis 12:2-3:

> *"I will make you into a great nation and I will bless you; I will make your name great, and you will be a blessing. I will bless those who bless you, and whoever curses you I will curse, and all the peoples on earth will be blessed through you" (NIV).*

This was God's promise to Abram(ham), and African Americans are his descendants. Current, modern-day support to Israel is based upon this scripture.

Now, reimagine that "you" are the "great nation" referred to here and not those currently residing in Israel. What does this mean to you? How does this text, taken literally in this lifetime, affect you? Currently, it may seem that African Americans are being cursed, but according to this same scripture, those who cursed them will face the consequences.

We find the certainty of that promise in the book written to the Hebrews:

> *"When God made his promise to Abraham, since there was no one greater for him to swear by, he swore by himself, saying; 'I will surely bless you and give you many descendants" (Hebrews 6:13-14 NIV).*

God swore by Himself! He is the greatest and highest authority. This is sealed in who He is, and we know He does not lie. He keeps His Word. Man, on the other hand, cannot make that claim or such a promise – because he does not have the power to make it happen. Even with the best intentions, we fall short. That is not the case with God. Therefore, we cannot base our human standards of belief in God on our standards of belief in man. There is no comparison.

It may be hard to grasp this concept because it is the opposite of what we have experienced. Promises are made and broken before we can even hope for them to happen. Similarly, many African Americans find it hard to trust anyone – because their trust has often been violated. Consequently, when they hear the truth, it seems impossible because they have learned to survive and function amid distrust. The system in place, which promises to protect African Americans from criminals, instead criminalizes them. The so-called system in place to protect them locks them up for life, throws away the key, and labels them criminals. They find themselves locked in the judicial system of the land, which does not work on their behalf. The system designed to educate them does not teach them and leaves them behind – not just in the United States but globally. The medical system designed to keep them healthy – refuses to provide adequate health care. Yes, African Americans have reason to doubt man's promises – so they must trust in the promises of God. Without that trust, there is no hope. Without hope, there is little to cling to. But that hope must be in the right place.

African Americans must learn and trust the scriptures and get to know God through His Word and prayer, both corporately and individually. Believe me, I get it. It is not easy or even normal in this life to trust someone you do not know.

The only way to get to know the true and living God is by spending time with Him. That is what one does in any relationship-building endeavor. You spend time with the person to get to know one another. The more time you spend, the more intimate the relationship becomes. To believe what God says in His Word and what He speaks through His Word requires a desire to get to know him. His Word is full of promises – promises that He keeps.

How do we know that He will keep His promises? We see them fulfilled in scripture. For example, in Exodus 7:4, God tells Moses that he will lay his hand on Egypt with mighty acts of judgment and bring the Israelites out of Egypt – and He did just that!

See – once you get the truth into your spirit and read and study God's Word, you will see Him in a totally different light. For one, He is not some distant God to a group of people He has no regard for. That is a lie straight from the pit of hell. African Americans, you are His own. You are His chosen people. Reunite with Him. He called you out of the darkness and lies of this world into the marvelous light of His truth and love. You must re-learn to put your trust in Him.

When the Hebrews get on one accord and bless the Lord – When we return to Him – standing on, trusting, and believing His word – Oh, what a time that will be! That is the fear of the oppressors - knowing the power that will come upon this peculiar community. I say "when" this happens intentionally – because it will happen. How can I be so confident? I have read His Word, and I trust and believe it.

God knows where we are! Do not be deceived.

> "In that day the Lord will extend his hand yet a second time to recover the remnant that remains of his people, from Assyria, from Egypt, from Pathros, from Cush, from Elam, from Shinar, from Hamath, and from the coastlands of the sea. He will raise a signal for the nations and will assemble the banished of Israel and gather the dispersed of Judah from the four corners of the earth" (Isaiah 11:11-12 ESV).

God is forgiving!

> "Behold, the days are coming, declares the LORD, when I will make a new covenant with the house of Israel and the house of Judah, not like the covenant that I made with their fathers on the day when I took them by the hand to bring them out of the land of Egypt, my covenant that they broke, though I was their husband, declares the LORD. For this is the covenant that I will make with the house of Israel after those days, declares the LORD: I will put my law within them, and I will write it on their hearts. And I will be their God, and they shall be my people. And no longer shall each one teach his neighbor and each his brother, saying, 'Know the LORD,' for they shall all know me, from the least of them to the greatest, declares the LORD. For I will forgive their iniquity, and I will remember their sin no more" (Jeremiah 31:31-34 ESV).

CHAPTER TEN

HIDDEN IDENTITY OF THE HEBREW PEOPLE

There have been some subtle and some not-so-subtle attempts to hide the identity of the original Hebrew people. This practice started in Biblical times and continues today. When the Negros exited the slave ships, part of their indoctrination into the "new land" was deliberately forming and molding them into the land's religion, which was a twisted version of Christianity. The parallel priority was to strip them of their identity. This was done strategically and systematically until the indoctrination was complete. There are several aspects to it, but we will focus on the following:

Misuse of Scripture - Scriptures such as 1 Peter 2:18 were used by slave masters to justify their actions. It reads:

> *"Slaves, submit yourselves to your masters with all respect, not only to those who are good and considerate; but also, to those who are harsh" (NIV).*

In some of today's modernized versions of the Bible, the word "slaves" has been translated to "servants." However, during that time of Biblical history, it is estimated that half the Roman population were slaves. It does not mean the Bible tolerates slavery. It was a reality of that time, culture, and rule of the tyrannical empowered government in place.

Changing of Names: One of the first things worth noting was the changing of the names of Hebrew slaves when they arrived in America and stepped off those slave ships. This was not a new practice. Notably, in the story of the fiery furnace, the four Hebrew boys' names were changed by the Babylonian King who captured them. The names were changed to reflect the culture they were in; (Belteshazzar, Shadrach, Meshach and Abednego). The practice of changing names was the same practice followed in slavery with the so-called African Americans. This provides a quick way to strip someone of their identity. Isn't it interesting that the names given to African Americans have never satisfied the people as a whole? The names given to African Americans or selected by them as cultural identity was sought, were never sufficient. They never will be because it is not who we are. We were Black, Afro-Americans, African Americans, Colored, Niggers – everything but our true ancestry name – Hebrews.

As a visual – you may recall the scene from the movie "Roots" where Kunta Kinte – a captive of American slavery, was beaten into submission to accept his name change. After the cruel and severe beatings, he came to a point of submission and accepted the name given him – "Toby". While the story was fictional – the practice was real. Names had meaning and connected people to a region, ancestry, or tribe.

The changing of names did not occur with just people, but with Biblical markers, as well. These markers could connect or identify a people within an area, or a region known by name or easily identifiable by the inhabitants of the area. This was also an effective way to hide identity. Therefore, as you read the Bible and look for something in its historical context – you will not find it without digging deep into specific commentaries or buried resources that can translate the information for you.

God changed names to change character: Abram to Abraham. Saul to Paul. Sarai to Sarah. Simon to Peter. Names have meaning – then and now. This knowledge presents an opportunity for African Americans to be cognizant of the names we give our children. Let's give our children names that speak life or greatness into their souls.

Separating and Breaking up the Family: This was another practice with deliberate intentions. When an infant or child was separated from their family, they had no concrete knowledge of their identity as they grew into childhood and then adulthood. In time as they had children – multiplying the degrees of separation - there was nothing to tell their offspring except to provide them with the last name of the slave owner or the geographic region they were from – as though it was their place of origin.

It is pure joy when African Americans can trace their ancestry back to a tribe in Africa, and this has only been more accessible through the access of modern-day DNA testing. Many African Americans' ancestry ends on the plantation from which their forefathers and mothers were enslaved. For others, it has been reduced simply to a state or region within the U.S., for example, Florida, Georgia, South Carolina, Alabama, or Louisiana, etc. This, to me, has been one of the greatest – and deliberate – dismantling of the connectedness of the Black (Hebrew) family structure.

However, one thing that was not erased was their connection to God. Slaves knew the stories of the Bible, and slaves who were able, for whatever reason afforded them, learned to speak English by reading the 1611 original King James Version of the Bible. I believe that is where Ebonics originated! Read it, and you will see what I mean.

They also sang songs about Moses and Jericho that were not taught to them by their slave owners. They brought forth their memory of tribal knowledge. Harriet Tubman was nicknamed Moses because they knew of God's deliverance of the Hebrews out of Egypt. They drew on that knowledge and hope in Him to deliver them from American bondage.

The conspiracy to change, alter, and hide the identity of the "Hebrew" slaves was effective.

REFLECTIONS

_____

_____

_____

_____

_____

_____

_____

_____

_____

_____

_____

_____

_____

_____

_____

_____

_____

_____

_____

_____

_____

_____

CHAPTER ELEVEN

ACTIONS TO ERADICATE HEBREW HISTORY OF AFRICAN AMERICANS - INCLUDING BIBLICAL

A s you read the following information, allow it to begin reprogramming your mind toward liberation. Let it serve as an illumination of truth that will lead you out of dark thinking. African Americans have lived long enough with the false narrative of who they are and who they believe themselves to be as a people. Based on that narrative, this includes the oppression, hatred, and continued disenfranchisement they have faced for centuries. So, the false narrative of who and what became the accepted "known". Now, the "how" is what needs to be explored. It is time to let the light of truth prevail. This chapter will help break through the vaulted walls of subliminal strongholds – still unknown to many in the African American Community. It will help in understanding how we got where we are!

Let's examine some calculated psychological practices that were successful in design and application. It helps shed light on the "how" questions that have or have not been asked or answered.

The William Lynch Letter

In 1712 a writing attributed to a man named William Lynch presented a philosophy to slave owners on how to control their slaves. Keep in mind the first slave ships arrived in Jamestown, VA, in 1619 – some 93 years before his address.

I have selected some quotes from this writing for the sole purpose of helping us understand the depth of this action. However, it is not my intent, under any circumstances to promote this propaganda. It is provided for root-cause analyses only. The information could make one wonder why, after nine decades of slavery, such drastic and evil practices were needed.

QUOTE 1: *"I have a foolproof method for controlling your black slaves. I guarantee every one of you that if it is installed correctly, it will control the slaves for at least 300 years."* Another comment says possibly a thousand years – and we are now over 400 years into this teaching – which is extremely detailed. In my opinion, William Lynch's philosophy was a method of mind control.

QUOTE 2: *"We must completely annihilate the mother tongue of both the new nigger and the new mule and institute a new language that involves the new life's work of both. You know language is a peculiar institution. It leads to the heart of a people. The more a foreigner knows about another country's language, the more he can move through all levels of that society."* One might liken this to the Tower of Babel, albeit with evil intent. Strip them of their language because it strips them of their identity. It strips them of their mother tongue, which is Hebrew. God preserved the Hebrew tongue for the Hebrew people when he scattered the nations and gave them new languages.

QUOTE 3: *"We reversed nature by burning and pulling a civilized nigger apart and bullwhipping the others to the point of death, all in her presence. By her being left alone, unprotected, with the MALE IMAGE DESTROYED, the ordeal caused her to move from her psychologically dependent state to a frozen, independent state. In this frozen, psychological state of independence, she will raise her MALE and female offspring in reversed roles. For FEAR of the young male's life, she will psychologically train him to be MENTALLY WEAK and DEPENDENT, but PHYSICALLY STRONG. Because she has become psychologically independent, she will train her FEMALE offspring to be psychologically independent. What have you got? You've got the nigger WOMAN OUT FRONT AND THE nigger MAN BEHIND AND SCARED."* This method equates to trauma and paralyzing fear! Success does not separate you; it classifies you as "civilized." But that classification does not insulate you or separate you from all the others.

QUOTE 4: *"Don't forget, you must pitch the OLD black male versus the YOUNG black male, and the YOUNG black male against the OLD black male. You must use the DARK skin slaves verses the LIGHT skin slaves, and the LIGHT skin slaves verses the DARK skin slaves. You must use the FEMALE versus the MALE, and the MALE versus the FEMALE. You must also have white servants and overseers who distrust all blacks. But it is NECESSARY THAT YOUR SLAVES TRUST AND DEPEND ON US. THEY MUST LOVE, RESPECT, AND TRUST ONLY US. Gentlemen, these kits are your keys to control."* Keys to control that are still working; in fact, they have become the norm. A friend shared a conversation she had with a non-African American colleague. He asked her why black men do not marry the women they are with. Why don't they get married? Well, I submit this as an answer, psychological control! The family structure is opposite the indoctrination.

African Americans were in a land far away – with people who didn't look like them, talk like them, or understand them. These people were re-inventing and violently reinforcing the art and imagination of who they purposed them to be. There is more to this system, and with just these four quotes, I believe this clarifies why African Americans are so disjointed as a people. As this insidious plan unravels, it can begin to answer many familiar "why are African Americans … so" questions. It was part of the indoctrination into this new land.

This practice has proven successful in all aspects, in that African Americans were stripped of everything: Expressions of worship, heritage, ancestry, language, family with its structure, land, and memory.

That plan worked and is still working, but it is not eternal. African Americans have the power to turn it around. Change happens first by being reconciled to God, then to one another. When God fights battles, He does not lose! We have been fighting the wind, one by one, in our own strength. That will not work. When we come together on one accord – there will be a shift. Some brave soldiers were taken from the African American community – which seemingly left a feeling of hopelessness, defenselessness, and despair. Our anointed and appointed leaders cannot be on the battlefield alone. The community will have to hold up their leaders' arms in battle – until the victory is won. We will need prayer warriors praying – while the soldiers are fighting. God will need to hear our unified cries for help. We will need to put on the full armor of God – and go into this spiritual battle – trusting and believing the victory is already won.

There is a shift happening now. There awaits a full victory for those prepared to endure to the end.

In the movie *Black Panther*, a statement was made regarding the city Wakanda; *"If the world found out what we truly are; what we possess, we could lose our way of life."* In the case of the scattered Hebrews, this is a good thing! We would lose the current way of life and live more like the fictitious Wakanda.

African Americans certainly have the brainpower to do so. Memorize this verse from Deuteronomy 7:6:

> *"The Lord Your God has chosen you out of all the peoples on the face of the earth to be his people, his treasured possession." (NIV)*

Census Records Mysteriously Burned

The 1890 Census Records stored in the basement of a building sustained severe waterlog and smoke damage from two different fires. The first fire occurred in 1896, and the second one in 1921. My great grandfather should have been in that Census. I cannot find him. In 1930, the records were permanently destroyed. There were different accounts of what caused the fire, including conspiracy theories, but regardless – the records were permanently destroyed. The so-called African American (Hebrew) slaves were officially counted in 1870, which according to Archives.gov, provided the first official last name, age, place of birth, and relationships within the family. That occurred 251 years after Hebrews arrived in the United States. Without any official government record (as opposed to private records), the transfer of identity was able to take place. At this point, the "place of birth" was the United States of America – not Africa with no connections.

After the original slaves died, there would no longer be the ability to privately provide an oral transfer of history to their children and children's children, provided they were not separated. Without historical reference, the Hebrew's identity was lost, and the imposed identity was associated to a Plantation with the last name of the slave owner. Checkmate – New Identity!

Black Hebrews Living in Jerusalem Today

We have established that Black Hebrews are living in Jerusalem today. This information is readily accessible online.

Interestingly, I have seen select images of them that would make one believe they are helpless orphans. Do not believe the hype. They are Hebrews, and they are black. They are living in Jerusalem – the Promised Land.

Haiti

On January 1, 1804, Haiti gained their freedom from slavery and independence from Colonial rule. As a result, the West dismantled its empire. Today we hear them referenced by some awful names. They could not eradicate them physically, so they did it economically and politically by cutting them off from the rest of the free world.

Based on the painted picture of Haitians and the conditions publicized, the "good life" other black people have become accustomed to living, would make it undesirable to be associated with them. It is more appealing to be associated with a plantation owner! I am not stating this as a personal belief but highlighting the sinister ways our minds have been controlled. Begin the mental deprogramming process. Without that, moving forward will take another 400+ years.

Pictures from Catholic Compound in Kenya

The author took the following pictures on a Missions Trip to Kenya on the grounds of a Catholic Compound there. They are presented for your review and consideration.

*Photos by: Jocelyn D. Whitehead

These are only two photos of many taken at the complex. What does this say to you? Why are these sculptures on the grounds of a Catholic compound in Africa depicting known Biblical characters and sacred moments in the life of Christ? Why are they reflected as people of color? Is it because they take it for granted in the same manner, we take the images that have been indoctrinated into us for granted?

When I witnessed this, my eyes were just opening to the fuller revelation of what I know now — to what I accept as the truth. It would be hard to pass the image of the art and imagination of Michelangelo's mind in his famous portrait of Christ that the western world has accepted, in Kenya. During my visits to Kenya, seeing someone without dark skin was a rarity. That is who they are – beautiful dark-skinned people – with a known identity, at least to their motherland.

The following picture is a Mosaic in a church in Nairobi, Kenya. It is interesting to note the different skin tones and facial features depicted in each person.

*Photo by: Jocelyn D. Whitehead

African Americans have history. They just need to be introduced to it. A good place to start would be reading the Bible. The history of the Hebrews is our history. What is not captured in schoolbooks is in the Bible.

REFLECTIONS

_____

_____

_____

_____

_____

_____

_____

_____

_____

_____

_____

_____

_____

_____

_____

_____

_____

_____

_____

_____

_____

_____

_____

_____

_____

_____

_____

CHAPTER TWELVE

MODERN DAY
JEWISH COMMUNITY

A logical question that may arise is if African Americans (and others) are the original Hebrews, who are the people classified as Jews throughout the world? Great question!

First, I must emphasize this is about the lost identity of the original Hebrew people to who they really are. It does not intend to disregard or diminish all other Jewish communities. It seeks to give proper placement of a peculiar people - disconnected from their ancestral roots.

This is a progressive revelation that will be fully revealed in God's appointed time and season.

However, based on my extensive research and study, DNA documentations, and Biblical truths, I believe African Americans and others in the Islands of black and brown color are the original Hebrews.

Yes, the question of who the current Jews are is a valid one and the answer varies depending on the reference or source explored.

This information in no way diminishes the horrific crimes of the Holocaust and the hatred experienced in the world. It simply answers a question about lineage of the original Hebrew people.

For broader information on this topic, there are additional sources available to consult for expanded research.

REFLECTIONS

_____

_____

_____

_____

_____

_____

_____

_____

_____

_____

_____

_____

_____

_____

_____

_____

_____

_____

_____

CHAPTER THIRTEEN

SCRIPTURE — THE EVIDENCE

Listed below are a few select scriptures supportive of the true Hebrew identity.

SCRIPTURE REFERENCE	TEXT	RELEVANCE
Deuteronomy 4:27, 28:15-68	"The Lord will scatter you among the peoples, and only a few of you will survive among the nations to which the Lord will drive you."	Details the Plight
1 Chronicles 16:13	"...You his servants, the descendants of Israel, his chosen ones, the children of Jacob."	Seed of Jacob...Chosen Ones
Deuteronomy 28:64	"Then the Lord will scatter you among all nations, from one end of the earth to the other. There you will worship other gods— gods of wood and stone, which neither you nor your ancestors have known."	Scattered/Not Lost
Baruch 2:30; 4:6 (Apocrypha)	"You were sold to the nations, not for your destruction, but because you moved God to wrath; thus, you were delivered to your enemies."	Corporate Sin of Hebrews
Psalm 105:5(b)-6; 42	"Remember the wonders he has done, his miracles, and the judgments he pronounced, you his servants, the descendants of Abraham, his chosen ones, the children of Jacob." "For he remembered his holy promise given to his servant Abraham."	Unfolding of Word gives light & imparts understanding
Psalm 83:1-4	"O God do not remain silent; do not turn a deaf ear, do not stand aloof, O God. See how your enemies growl, how your foes rear their heads. With cunning they conspire against your people; they plot against those you cherish. "Come," they say, "let us destroy them as a nation, so that Israel's name is remembered no more."	Conspiracy against Israel

SCRIPTURE REFERENCE	TEXT	RELEVANCE
Isaiah 29:22; 41:8	"Therefore, this is what the Lord, who redeemed Abraham, says to the descendants of Jacob: "No longer will Jacob be ashamed; no longer will their faces grow pale, "But you, Israel, my servant, Jacob, whom I have chosen, you descendants of Abraham my friend...""	Hope/Promise
Jeremiah 15:14; 17:4	"I will enslave you to your enemies in a land you do not know, for my anger will kindle a fire that will burn against you."	Judgment on His people.
Joel 3:6	"You sold the people of Judah & Jerusalem to the Greeks that you might send them far from their homeland."	Result of Disobedience
Ezekiel 6:8-10	"But I will spare some, for some of you will escape the sword when you are scattered among the lands and nations." Then in the nations where they have been grieved by their adulterous hearts, which have turned away from me, and by their eyes, which have lusted after their idols."	Judgement
2 Corinthians 11:21-22	"Whatever anyone else dares to boast about—I am speaking as a fool—I also dare to boast about. Are they Hebrews? So am I. Are they Israelites? So am I. Are they Abraham's descendants? So am I."	Paul's Heritage as Hebrew
Luke 21:24	"They will fall by the sword and will be trampled on by the Gentiles until the times of the Gentiles are fulfilled."	Destiny
Book of Hebrews	Author generally stated as unknown. Biblical book written specifically to the Hebrews. Should be titled: *A Letter to the Hebrew People.*	Written specifically to Christian Jews in the New Testament of the Bible who were ready to throw in the towel and go back to Judaism because of the severe persecution they were under due to following Christianity.

*All Scripture references in chart are taken from the NIV.

When you read the scriptures from now on, read them with a sense of urgency in light of the truth!

CHAPTER FOURTEEN

OVERLOOKED — VISIBLE FACTS

Unveiling the truth of who African Americans are and their inclusive place in history is daunting. Thankfully, some information is hiding in open view. Let's examine a few of them:

First, let us look at the description of Jesus in Revelation 1:14-15;

"The hairs of his head were white, like white wool, like snow. His eyes were like a flame of fire, his feet were like burnished bronze, refined in a furnace, and his voice was like the roar of many waters" (ESV).

Ugh! Let's think about that. We should go have a V8! His hair was white like "wool." Wool comes from sheep. Sheep's wool (or hair) is kinky and curly. It is thick and robust. It is not straight and stringy. Next, His feet were like burnished bronze. Burnished bronze in color is like chocolate brown.

The key is the adjective 'burnished', which makes it different from a copperish tone. However, even with that, it is a hue of brown.

Daniel 7:9 – gives us a prophetic vision of Jesus:

*"As I looked, thrones were placed, and the Ancient of
Days took his seat; his clothing was white as snow,
and the hair of his head like pure wool; his throne was
fiery flames; its wheels were burning fire" (ESV).*

Notice Daniel's description; *"his head like pure wool..."* Here we have another description of Jesus' hair. And isn't society's fixation on African Americans' hair interesting? It's too kinky. Certain styles are too ethnic. It is to this or to that! What is all the fuss about African American hair? Is it too fitting of the description of Christ's hair?

Acts 8:26-39 – The Ethiopian Eunuch. All references in the Bible to Ethiopia = Black. Ethiopians are descendants of Cush (Noah's son Ham). Cush is translated as "black". There are varying opinions of the Ethiopians in that there appears to have been a long-term intermixing of nationalities during Biblical times. Still, one consistent thing is their skin color – it is "dark." So, any reference to Ethiopia is "black." This Eunuch was a court official to the Ethiopian Queen – Candace. Additionally, there are Black Ethiopian Jews in Africa and Israel today.

Jeremiah 13:23(a):

*"Can the Ethiopian change his skin or the leopard his
spots?" (ESV)*

Now that is God himself speaking matter-of-factly to prove a point. Their skin is black, and it is permanent. They cannot change it, nor can a leopard change his spots – it is what it is.

Queen of Sheba – She is the Queen who traveled to meet King Solomon (David's son) and ultimately had a son by him. Ethiopians claim that she is Ethiopian, and others claim that she was from Arabia – which is a more modern interpretation. She has traditionally been associated with Ethiopia – which is black. Her son, Menelik, is said to have been the king of the royal dynasty of his father, Solomon, in Ethiopia. This 3000-year Ethiopian dynasty / monarchy lasted until 1975 with the death of Ethiopia's last Emperor, Haile Selassie, who always maintained this position. The story is still alive, though.

Samson – This truly speaks for itself in Judges 16:13:

> *"Then Delilah said to Samson, "Until now you have mocked me and told me lies. Tell me how you might be bound." And he said to her, "If you* **weave** *the* **seven locks** *of my head with the web and fasten it tight with the pin, then I shall become weak and be like any other man" (ESV).*

Other versions of the Bible say "seven braids" instead of locks. *At any rate, braids or locks are not straight or stringy hair!* Herodotus described the ancient Egyptians as Black with – Wooly Hair. This description seems unusual when we look at the current Egyptians, but consider the following text in Exodus 14:13:

> *"And Moses said to the people, "Fear not, stand firm, and see the salvation of the* LORD*, which he will work for you today. For the Egyptians whom you see today, you shall never see again" (ESV).*

The original Egyptians were dark-skinned, black people. Even when we look up ancient pictures, it is clear the Egyptians were dark-skinned, black people. One must travel outside of the United States of America to see and understand history. On some of the pyramids in Egypt, the noses are missing from the pharaohs' faces. The act hid a "black" identifying nose – a broad nose. Something that is undeniably associated with a particular race of people.

The respected Jewish Historian Josephus gives additional information regarding God's prepping of Moses for his battle with Pharoah, and he says:

> "After this God had Moses put his right hand into his bosom. He obeyed, and when he took it out, it was white, and in color like chalk, but afterward it returned to its wanted color again (Josephus, 1987, p.12)."

The question then becomes, what is the "wanted color"? At the time Josephus wrote this, it would have been clearly understood. Leprosy was another occasion in Biblical times where a person's skin would "became leprous – white as snow." What color was it before it was turned white? Why was it such a big deal that it turned white?

History has been white-washed and African Americans have been brain-washed!

CHAPTER FIFTEEN

THE SLAVE TRADE

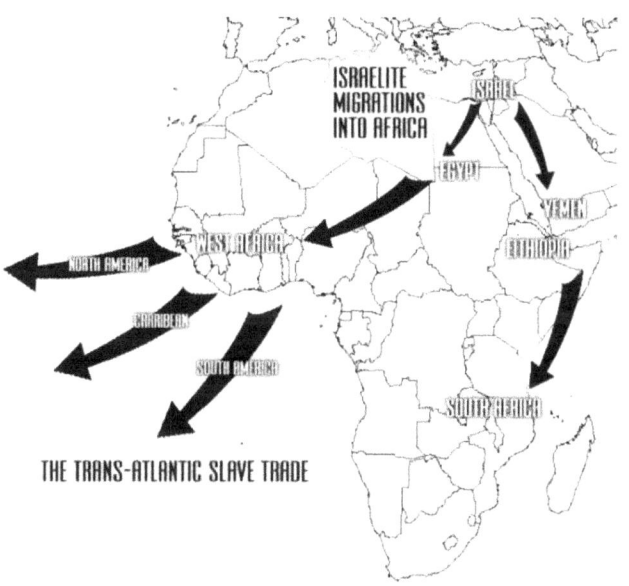

et's take a moment and briefly look at the early start of the slave trade industry. Early slave trading started with local Arabs and transformed into an Institution of Slavery by the Portuguese. Around 1445 the Portuguese began expanding their territories and discovered that the gold commodity they sought was less profitable than trading human beings. It became big business for them.

An interesting thing occurred. Pope Nicholas, the 5th, allowed the King of Portugal to legalize slavery. He allowed the king, in writing to do the following:

"... invade, search out, capture, vanquish and subdue all Saracens and pagans whatsoever, and other enemies of Christ, whatsoever placed, and the kingdoms, dukedoms, principalities, dominions, possessions and all movable and immovable goods whatsoever held and possessed by them to reduce their persons to **perpetual slavery**.*" (KingdomPreppers.org).*

Now, it baffles the mind to even conceptualize one person of flesh, telling another person of flesh they have the right to the flesh of yet another for the sole purpose of commodity, while placing themselves in God's seat of judgment.

Subsequently, Spain, Britain, France, the Dutch, Canada, and the U.S. participated in the slave trade. Many hands were dirtied in this ruthless act against humanity.

Many played a key role in the capturing and ultimate marketing of slavery. Included are the Jewish community as well as other dark-skinned people in the region. Though they deny involvement, it can be validated[1]. Noteworthy: There was an element of black-on-black crime! That did not just start today. The significant difference is in Heritage – not skin color. This information is significant because it adds a missing piece to the puzzle. The Hebrews are the Chosen People of God. Their haters are widespread. The selling out was based on who they were – distinctively different in Heritage – though significantly alike in appearance.

The Slave Trade in America was one of the most barbaric and egregious assaults on humanity for the sake of capitalism in modern history. Men, women, and children were treated worse than animals. Families were destroyed. The captured slaves' cultures were denied and re-written. The captors stripped the slaves of everything they had and forced them into a culture they had no prior knowledge of, with people unfamiliar to them.

---

1   https://blackhistory938.wordpress.com/2017/06/06/the-hebrew-israelites-and-the-trans-atlantic-slave-trade-connection/

Slavery in America was an act that has continued to plague the United States of America for over 400 years now.

But the Hebrews were warned of that in Jeremiah 16:13:

> "So I will throw you out of this land into a land
> neither you nor your ancestors have known,
> and there you will serve other gods day and
> night, for I will show you no favor" (NIV).

How about Jeremiah 15:14 (a):

> "I will enslave you to your enemies in a
> land you do not know..." (NIV).

Just in case you are wondering why God would do this, Jeremiah 5:19 (BSB) helps us to understand it better:

> "And when the people ask, 'For what offense has
> the LORD our God done all these things to us?' You
> are to tell them, 'Just as you have forsaken Me and
> served foreign gods in your land, so will you serve
> foreigners in a land that is not your own.'" (BSB).

This land in America was foreign to the Hebrew people and still is today in some ways to African Americans. So, we need not get too comfortable here anyway!

A 1960s hit song by The Impressions resonated with me as I wrote this book. I remembered the hook line but not the entire lyrics. Let's examine the words:

> "People get ready, there's a train a comin'.
> Don't need no baggage, you just get on board. All you
> need is faith to hear the diesels hummin'. You don't need
> no ticket; you just thank the Lord. So, people get ready
> for the train to Jordan, picking up passenger's coast
> to coast. Faith is the key, open the doors and board

em; there's hope for all - among those loved the most.
There ain't no room for the hopeless sinners, who would
hurt all mankind just to save his own, believe me now.
Have pity on those whose chances grow thinner, for
there's no hiding place against the kingdom's throne.
So, People get ready – there's a train a comin' – don't
need no baggage, you just get on board. All you need
is faith to hear the diesels hummin'. You don't need
no ticket; you just thank the Lord" (Mayfield, 1965).

Now that was as prophetic as it gets! The amazing thing is it was a 1960s R&B (Rhythm & Blues) song, during The Civil Rights Movement. Nevertheless, it would reach everyone. African Americans' train is coming – the diesels are hummin' - get ready! Get on board.

In 1897 The Houston Post published the following very interesting article. The title reads; *"1897: Educated African Jewish Man is conceptually Confusing to Americans* (Post, 2021)."

NEGRO WHO CAN WRITE HEBREW.

He Is Deaf and Dumb and Comes From an African Town.

Hartford, Conn., September 19.—A young African negro has been in this city for the last few days who claims to be a Hebrew. He is deaf and dumb and as black as the ace of spades.

He carries a pad of paper with him and answers all questions by writing them in Hebrew and Loschen Khodish. What excites the most wonder is that he writes Loschen Khodish very rapidly. It is the language of the books of Moses, and is made a special study of, spoken and written with ease only by the rabbis and highly educated Hebrews.

The negro was sent to one of the rabbis of Hartford, who is perfectly satisfied that he is a Hebrew. He says that he came from a large town in Africa, where there is a tribe of about 20,000 black Hebrews who speak Loschen Khodish and are quite prosperous. He also says that his father is a rabbi in that town, and that is why his father took the trouble to teach him to write these languages, which needed an extra amount of labor on account of his being deaf and dumb.

He says his people not only write Loschen Khodish, but it is their speaking language as well. He left home a few years ago and has seen a good deal of the world. In each town he hunts up the Jewish section, and there they give him lodging, food and money.

What surprises him, he writes, is that no Hebrew knows of his countrymen in Africa.

This article is so powerful. Let's break it down.

Title: *Negro Who Can Write Hebrew*. Ok – not a mystery. He is Hebrew, and he is black! That is his native tongue. He did not learn that in America! Notice it says, *"it is the language of the books of Moses."*

Subtitle: *He is Deaf and Dumb and Comes from an African Town*. The absurdity of the irony. First, it states he can write Hebrew, which means he can read! Then the article says he carries a pad of paper with him and answers all questions by writing them in Hebrew and Loschen Khodish.[2] Sounds to me like he was bi-lingual.

Next, the article states his father is a Rabbi in Africa and taught him *"these languages"* – which the article says took longer to teach him because he is deaf and dumb.

2 Loschen Khodish – One Interpretation: Holy Tongue

The last paragraph is powerful – *"What surprises him, he writes, is that no Hebrew knows of his countrymen in Africa."* He recognized his Hebrew countrymen in America and that they had no clue who they were.

It appears to me the Americans were the only ones confused! He communicated and clearly articulated his thoughts. This young, learned Hebrew though deaf and mute was quite articulate! The *Houston Post* used the archaic term for mute as dumb. An interesting play on words.

Another article on the same subject entitled, *A Colored Hebrew - A Negro Mute Who Writes Loschen Khodish*, was also published on September 14,1897 in The Hartford Courant. The articles are basically the same, with the Hartford Courant providing more narrative as it appears he was in Connecticut.

They write, *"He has traveled the world, says he came from a large town in Africa where there are a tribe of about 20,000 black Hebrews who speak Loschen Khodish, and he was trying to raise funds to go home to Africa."* Additionally, he seeks the Jewish section of whatever town he visits. They challenge his claim to be Hebrew stating; *"If he is what he represents himself to be and if what he claims is true, he is quite an interesting character."* But it is the last line of this article that struck me which states; *"That he is a Hebrew no Hartford Hebrew who has seen him has a shadow of doubt."* That includes the Rabbi they sent him to, to confirm his claims.

CHAPTER SIXTEEN

FOUR HUNDRED YEARS

Acts 7:6-10

Whe I first read the following text, I was overwhelmed once again with the striking similarities to the condition of African Americans as a population in America. This is simply astounding.

"God spoke to him in this way: 'For four hundred years your descendants will be strangers in a country not their own, and they will be enslaved and mistreated. But I will punish the nation they serve as slaves,' God said, 'and afterward they will come out of that country and worship me in this place.' Then he gave Abraham the covenant of circumcision. And Abraham became the father of Isaac and circumcised him eight days after his birth. Later Isaac became the father of Jacob, and Jacob became the father of the twelve patriarchs.

"Because the patriarchs were jealous of Joseph, they sold him as a slave into Egypt. But God was with him and rescued him from all his troubles. He gave Joseph wisdom and enabled him to gain the

*goodwill of Pharaoh king of Egypt. So, Pharaoh made
him ruler over Egypt and all his palace" (NIV).*

Consider the following 400-year journey in America.

1619 – 1st Hebrews (Negroes) Landed in Jamestown
+ 400 – Years of Slavery*[1]
=2019 - (End of 400 Years).

The African American journey in this land is ending. As African Americans await God's timing for deliverance, there are many signs that time is drawing nigh.

When I say our journey has ended – that is not to say we are getting ready to get back on ships and return to the promised land. However, what is ending is mental slavery. The younger generation has a special calling and grace (upon them) to rise as leaders. Hebrews are emerging like never before in leadership and visible roles all over the world. God is preparing the hearts of the elect as He begins to remove the veil that has surrounded the truth of who African Americans are as a people. Not everyone will get it – until it happens – but many hearts will be prepared in the process to receive it at the given time. Doors of opportunity are opening for African Americans (Hebrews) that have been closed, destroyed, or burned down previously. This timing is not a coincidence– it is Godincidence.

The contempt we have been under is beginning to lift. Compassion is slowly seeping into the hearts of people worldwide. We glimpsed what is to follow in 2021 with the outcry of support worldwide for the same things ignored for 400 years regarding the senseless and cold-blooded murder of an unarmed black man. There will always be hatred – that is just a fact – but African Americans will not always be mistreated.

---

1 The US Government has initiated a bill that will celebrate or recognize the 400 years since so called Africans were brought to America, which is, in all actuality, confirmation to this scripture. (HR1242 – 400 Years of African American History Commission Act).

Jesus says of himself, *"They hated me without cause"* (John 15:25). Hate has no rationality because it is birthed in a place of darkness.

Sometimes that darkness is so thick you cannot see your way through. Josephus describes the plague of darkness in Exodus as being so thick it was terrifying and immobilizing. He says the Egyptians could not see their own bodies – so they were afraid to move at all. They froze in place!

In reading this account, I envisioned this "darkness" as being felt – yet untouchable. The hatred waged against the Hebrew people is akin to this description of darkness. Darkness will come again, through hearts that will render the oppressors frozen.

Envy has been a problem with the Hebrews beginning early in Biblical times. We have come to discover that envy is at the root of many of their hardships. The Egyptians were envious of the Hebrews because of their prosperity, and they became very abusive to them and would come up with ways to inflict pain upon them. One of the ways they did this was by putting them to work through hard labor.

The Hebrews built cities, walls for the cities, and retaining walls for rivers to keep the water from overflowing into the cities. They were made to work to the point of collapse. No different than slavery in the United States. Yet even with this harsh labor and hostile work environment, the nation survived.

While the Egyptians sought to destroy them, the Hebrews were determined to ride it out. For 400 years, they endured this unjust – evil behavior. In Exodus Chapter 1, there was an attempt at genocide. Hebrew midwives were to kill other Hebrew children at birth if they were a boy. Then, by command of Pharoah, they were to throw all boys into the river. The annihilation of the Hebrew male began in Egypt and was, again, commanded by

King Herod in the New Testament of the Bible and continues today.

The more they were oppressed – the more they multiplied. As the comedian Robin Harris said, *"BeBe's kids don't die, they just multiply."*

One of the things digging in-depth to study this information does is highlight that African Americans have been down this road before. The history lesson lies in that they were delivered once before and will be delivered again. Pages from an old textbook were cut and applied in America. A textbook they were not privileged to read.

Of significance, we learn the more the Egyptians oppressed the Hebrews and increased their work to levels they felt would break them, it only strengthened them. It is no secret that African American employees have a more demanding or heavier workload than their peers in Corporate America. And guess what – just like in Egypt, it drives us to not only meet but exceed unrealistic demands. The work is often rewarded with more work – usually not financial recognition or promotion.

The same holds true for the attempts to suppress voting rights – to killing African American boys (and young men) – and what easier way than pin it on; black-on-black crime? Even though it is a convenient cover to hide under, the truth is that it was ingrained in them. However, when one knows the truth, they are poised to do better.

Each day the truth is being unveiled. Information will continue to come to light. It is necessary to reach the community in whatever or however many different formats it takes, as long as it is factual.

Four hundred (400) years is long enough for generations to be born and die, never knowing who they truly were. They would never know true freedom and never be able to love themselves because they were just a distant memory or passed down remnants of a story they could neither touch nor relate to. Nevertheless, African Americans suffered four hundred (400) years of their identity being rewritten for them — Four hundred (400) years of trying to conform to what was being placed on them while enduring what went against the grain of their own spirits.

Four hundred (400) years of bondage equates to four cycles of 100 years each. Four hundred years!

Yes, four hundred years is a long time, but it is not without an ending. There will be a second Exodus, and *"Pharaoh will have to Let God's People Go!"*

"When all these blessings and curses I have set before you come on you and you take them to heart wherever the LORD your God disperses you among the nations, and when you and your children return to the LORD your God and obey him with all your heart and with all your soul according to everything I command you today, then the LORD your God will restore your fortunes [or bring you back from captivity] and have compassion on you and gather you again from all the nations where he scattered you. Even if you have been banished to the most distant land under the heavens, from there the LORD your God will gather you and bring you back. He will bring you to the land that belonged to your ancestors, and you will take possession of it. He will make you more prosperous and numerous than your ancestors. The LORD your God will circumcise your hearts and the hearts of your descendants, so that you may love him with all your heart and with all your soul, and live" (Deuteronomy 30:1-6 NIV).

This text is pregnant with valuable information to lead and guide everyone into a state of awareness. This passage should prick hearts to dive into the deep waters of its meaning. Notice the opening line with the operative word *"when"*, indicating that it is going to happen. When African Americans [collectively] take their situation to heart, God will bring them home from wherever they have been dispersed. Home to himself in mind and spirit. The comforting hope is in verse 4, where God says even those scattered to the most distant parts of the earth will be brought back to the land that belonged to their ancestors. That land is not the United States, Jamaica, Haiti, West Indies, and other places – it is Jerusalem. This information has not been openly available to the hearing of African Americans for over 400 years. But God knows exactly who they are and where they are!

There is a beautiful story of a missionary, Mother Eliza George, a descendant of slaves, who dedicated her life to missionary work in Africa. When I say "dedicated her life, I mean her story is about *"real"* missionary work in the deepest remote areas of Africa - Liberia. In the Book on her life entitled; *When God Says Go* (Lutz, 2002), the following story is quoted from a resident in one of the villages.

> *"…When she told the people that she had come from across the sea, one of the old grandmothers placed her hand beside Mother's and said, 'Mammy, your hand looks just like my hand. You are my sister. They said long years ago that some of our people here took our brothers away across the water. We have been looking for our brothers to come back home. You are one of our sisters who has come back to us.'"*

As the history books continue to exclude African American history, oral teachings must be passed down to all the younger generations. As they become more educated and sophisticated in their knowledge, they must also seek understanding. Knowledge is a gift that comes with responsibility. It is not something to hoard or wear as a badge of honor to separate one another. We must share information freely. Once a person receives information, it is incumbent upon them what they do with it. The old saying applies. *"You can lead a horse to water, but you cannot make him drink."* When they are thirsty enough, they will drink.

This scripture brings tears to my eyes and hope to my soul. We all have a need to be connected.

My mother did not have a connection to her biological father, which left a silent voice of emptiness within her. She was unaware of any siblings from her father's side or where they resided. There was a disconnect in her ancestry that was never fulfilled and buried with her. Her known ancestry is only traceable through her maternal side.

This plight certainly is not exclusive to her. It is true throughout the history of many transported Hebrews to America. We have a silent voice of emptiness deep within as a people because we do not have full knowledge of our ancestry. We may or may not know something is missing but are clueless as to what it is. There is a longing to connect – to belong – to fit into a culture that does not accept us – yet tells us we must live according to the same standards of said culture. That is insanity!

Thus, even with the illusion of success, there is still a void inside the African American. Because we are constantly reminded, we are not accepted into the culture even after doing everything according to the rules. For every hurdle we successfully clear, an additional – higher one is added. That is why we may be so good in track and field; we have jumped some mighty hurdles in this land! We cannot stop. We are designed and equipped to succeed.

When God comes back for us – when He brings us back from our current psychological captivity, from everywhere we were scattered, it will be with love unmatched in Power.

REFLECTIONS

CHAPTER SEVENTEEN

HEBREWS

(As Titled in the Christian Bible)

"Hebrews," the title of a book in the Christian Bible, underwent a name change. In the 1611 original version of the King James Bible and subsequent Bibles, the Book is entitled; *"To the Hebrew People,"* or even more appropriately, *"Message to the Hebrew People."* The title is significant because it changes the whole psychological connectedness to a people. When you open this book and see "Hebrews," it becomes subjective to the reader. It appears to be an abstract Book placed near the back of the Bible – that includes, a wonderful tribute to a group of individuals strong in their faith. So much so it is referenced as the "Honor Roll of Faith." These individuals are Hebrews who did great things by faith.

In contrast, when the book reads; *"To the Hebrew People"* it gives an entirely different perspective. It is abundantly clear that it references a specific group of people. It is abundantly clear that there is a specific message to this group of people – who happen to be Jewish followers of Christ.

These Jewish Christians were being persecuted and were thinking of leaving the faith. The author (typically regarded as unknown) appears to be very familiar with the people.   He is encouraging them not to abandon the faith and does so by reminding them of their history. That history lesson also applies to African Americans today. Not to exclude anyone else but to highlight the connectedness to them.

The author walks the Hebrew Christians through their misunderstandings, beginning with the Superiority of Christ, the Son of God. He does this in the format of a great history lesson.

He then discusses Salvation and Jesus' superiority over the angels, reminding them of Psalm 8:4-6:

> "What is man that you are mindful of him, the Son of man that you care for him? You have made him a little lower than the heavenly beings and crowned him with glory and honor. You have given him dominion over the works of your hands, you have put all things under his feet" (ESV).

He discusses that Jesus is superior to Moses, debunking the thoughts and beliefs they were still holding onto, the Mosaic Law. The author breaks down the Priesthood from the Law into this era of Christ they are now in. He addresses the New Covenant under Jesus versus the Law. He talks about redemption under Christ and how Christs' sacrifice was superior to the Law in that Christs' sacrifice was once and for all as opposed to the sacrifice of countless animals.

He then helps the hearer to understand what Faith is and how it operates in this new dispensation of God's plan of redemption in Christ, not the Law.

It is a beautiful teaching and illustration for any student of the Bible to grasp the basic tenets of the Faith.

Curiously, how often have you been taught from this Book? To what basic teachings have you been introduced? Certainly

– the "Hall of Faith," found in Hebrews Chapter 11. However, there is so much more, especially as it relates to the people – specifically chosen by God as His very own.

The Letter to the Hebrew People must become to the African American – a study with the same fervor and intensity as the Torah was to the Israelites before Christ. Though scholars agree upon no specific author, it clearly is a love letter from God to His Chosen people. He lays out the historical context for which the Hebrews were to continue – in a manner that connects the Old to the New Covenant concisely and systematically.

This masterpiece is critical to understanding the connectedness of the Old and New Testaments, specifically as it relates to the Hebrews. It bridges the gap between those stuck in the Law of Moses, ushering them into the present time and space of God's grace. Hebrews is a well-documented and excellent history lesson, given in concise and understandable terms for the people to understand. That same revelation is waiting for all to grasp.

Hebrews 4:12 reads:

> "For the word of God is living and active, sharper than any double-edged sword, it penetrates even to dividing soul and spirit, joints, and marrow; it judges the thoughts and attitudes of the heart. Nothing in all creation is hidden from God's sight. Everything is uncovered and laid bare before the eyes of him to whom we must give account" (NIV).

To the Hebrews – learn your ancestral history.

REFLECTIONS

CHAPTER EIGHTEEN

TEN SIMILARITIES OF ENSLAVED HEBREWS IN EGYPT TO ENSLAVED HEBREWS IN AMERICA

When we consider the slavery of the Hebrews in Egypt and the Hebrews in America, there are some striking similarities. Let's compare a few of them:

1. The Hebrews were enslaved in Egypt for 430 years. The Hebrews have been in America for over 400 years, still awaiting God's timing.

2. Egyptian midwives were commanded to kill only the male children of Hebrew mothers. African American (Hebrew) males are being killed on American soil upon command.

3. The Egyptians had become lazy and greedy for gain at the benefit of other's labor. Americans became lazy and greedy for gain at the benefit of other's labor.

4. The Egyptians became envious of the Hebrews due to their wealth. Americans continuously destroyed the wealth of Hebrews in America. Most notably, but certainly

not isolated, the Oklahoma Massacre where what was once called "Black Wallstreet" was burned to the ground and the Hebrews had to flee. Fleeing was a state of being for Hebrews from the beginning – and it is still the case today.

5. Egyptians abused the Hebrews. America is still abusing the Hebrews.

6. Hebrews in Egypt had a love for labor. Hebrews in America have always been very hard working, even though the opposite title was given them.

7. Hebrew slaves built remarkable structures in Egypt. African American (Hebrew) slaves built remarkable structures in America.

8. Egyptian slaves were given tasks that were cruel and strenuous. African Americans (Hebrews) were made to work relentlessly in American fields and industry.

9. Hebrews in Egypt built the Pyramids. Hebrews in America built the White House.

10. God came down and rescued the Hebrews from Egyptian bondage. God will come down and rescue the African American (Hebrew) from American bondage and punish their oppressors just as He did with the Egyptian oppressors.

REFLECTIONS

_____

_____

_____

_____

_____

CHAPTER NINETEEN

CRUCIFIED AS THOUGH HIS BLACK LIFE DID NOT MATTER

When we consider the vicious attacks and cruelty against the Lord and Savior, Jesus the Christ, it helps to identify the parallel circumstances of Hebrews worldwide, but more specifically to the so-called African American (Hebrew). Jesus was falsely arrested on trumped-up charges and given a swift trial with the leaders of the day. Each one was aware he had done nothing wrong, yet He was tried by a jury of his haters and given a life sentence for something he did not do. The authorities tried to pressure Jesus into a plea deal. When Jesus refused to sign off on it, he was lied upon by false witnesses. After that, He was humiliated, verbally abused, stripped of his clothing, and spit upon. It didn't end there; his persecutors mocked, tortured, and made him carry his execution cross to a location where he was beaten beyond recognition. As he walked, they freely sucker-punched him in his face, slapped him – kicked him – flogged[1] him – and made the scene into a spectator sport. They hung him on a tree – stabbed him in his side, and watched him die while his mother, family, friends, and followers looked on.

---

1 Flogging involved beating a person with a whip that was made with small iron balls, or sharp pieces of sheep bones braided into leather straps. The whip would rip open the flesh – while the iron ball would bruise the body. The whip struck in a downward manner touching both sides of the back.

Now, if we pick apart this pattern they used on Jesus – it is the same thing imposed on African Americans – symbolically speaking.   First – he was falsely accused with trumped-up charges. There are countless cases of trumped-up charges still occurring today in the African American community. It began with false accusations against Jesus. Everything else was downhill from there. It did not matter what he said to defend himself; the judges did not hear him because he was already declared guilty. It did not matter that he was innocent. It did not matter that He was God in the flesh.   He was a Hebrew with power, authority, and position, and they wanted him off the scene.

He stood up to them intellectually, spiritually, and confidently. He stood His ground – and when you think about it – it truly is His ground! (Psalm 24:1) The Bible declares that the earth is the Lord's and everything in it. Now there are parallels to that as well. The authorities took His property along with His life – so they thought! Black Hebrew lives have been subject to abuse and mistreatment even before Jesus' physical human life on earth.

Jesus' crucifixion was the most brutal death that could be imposed on an individual. The system was designed for hardened criminals. When Jesus was brought before the authorities, one person acknowledged his innocence yet symbolically washed his hands of having anything to do with his death. However, you cannot wash innocent blood off your hands with a statement. So, he uses a technicality, deciding, instead, to turn him over to a different jurisdiction. Sound familiar?

At that time, there was a system in place that allowed one criminal to be released from the penalty of death. The leaders asked the crowd (that had already condemned Jesus) who they wanted to release – between Jesus and another man. They chose to release the guilty man and hang the innocent man. It does not take much imagination to realize this is still taking place today, as they shouted out, "Crucify Him"!

In those moments, Jesus's life did not matter. His deity did not matter. His innocence did not matter. The manner of death imposed on him did not matter. He was sentenced to death by crucifixion, and the authorities knew he was innocent. African Americans are still placed in these *"Catch-22"* situations where they get coerced into a false confession for a plea deal – or no deal with the promise of reduced charges; on charges that are false in the first place. It is a vicious cycle.

Jesus' life did matter, and because His life mattered – our lives matter. They matter to someone who has already gone before us and knows what you are going through. Jesus is the High Priest. In the Book, written to the Hebrew people, we read:

> *"For we do not have a high priest who is unable*
> *to sympathize with our weaknesses, but one*
> *who in every respect has been tempted as we*
> *are, yet without sin" (Hebrews 4:15 NIV).*

Jesus not only knows your pain; he carried it on that cross. He knows what African Americans have been through and are still going through because he has been there himself. His death on that cross, in turn, brought all an opportunity for eternal life with Him. It wasn't long after his death they realized they had made a big mistake! Their "bad" was huge.

His life mattered. His life still matters. Your life matters. Our lives matter.

REFLECTIONS

CHAPTER TWENTY

MOVE OF GOD

There is a movement happening in America relating to this information being unveiled. It is very important not to jump on any bandwagon. Study the Bible and align what is being taught to what God says in His Word. Do not abandon your Houses of Worship looking for "the church" teaching this information.

Some teachings on this subject are not sound. I'm reminded of the story of the Shepherds who were foretold of the birth of Jesus. When they arrived to see for themselves and share what was revealed to them to an assembled crowd of people, there was amazement. Mary, however, did not speak but it is recorded that she "pondered what was said in her heart." She did not fully understand at the time herself, though she knew in like manner as the Shepherds. This information is a progressive revelation.

The deity of Christ cannot be denied. The earthly heritage of Christ in human form renders him a Black Hebrew. Some say, why does that matter? I answer that with the same question. If it doesn't matter, then why not accept the truth?

Reject any notion that Christianity is a White man's religion. God is God of all people, but He did call a special people unto Himself – the Hebrews (Tribe of Judah).

Do not throw the baby out with the bath water. In other words, just because some of our Caucasian brothers may have put their spin on the Bible and fabricated some teachings beneficial to themselves, the basic tenets of the faith are the same. Do not discard what you have not studied, prayed over, and sought understanding for.

God is awakening His people to the call in 2 Chronicles 7:14:

"If my people who are called by My name will humble themselves, and pray and seek My face, and turn from their wicked ways, then I will hear from heaven, and will forgive their sin and heal their land" (NIV).

Pastor Omar Thibodeaux has a great truth that he taught to introduce this information; *"This is not about Theology – it is about Identity!"* Do not get that twisted.

What is the real identity of African Americans? It is time to drop all the fabricated labels and accept who we are in Christ – His chosen people. Yes, even God refers to the Hebrews as a peculiar people. A peculiar people special to God and His own possession. That is our identity African Americans. Embrace it.

God is moving, and we must move with his promptings. We must be clear; however, that the promptings are from Him.

Be sure you remain under sound Biblical Doctrine until God sends His anointed leader to deliver His people out of our current bondage. God raises leaders in every Divine endeavor He establishes.

The Hebrews had to wait on God to move on their behalf out of Egyptian bondage and other battles he fought for them. God had to prepare them first, mentally and physically. Then he instructed his anointed leader, Moses, to move on his command and in line with his instructions. God is the only one with the power to part a sea. Moving without Him will not render success.

We will know when that leader is established.

REFLECTIONS

_____

_____

_____

_____

_____

_____

_____

_____

_____

_____

_____

_____

_____

_____

_____

_____

_____

_____

_____

REFLECTIONS

_____

_____

_____

_____

_____

_____

_____

_____

_____

_____

_____

_____

_____

_____

_____

_____

_____

_____

_____

_____

_____

_____

_____

_____

_____

_____

_____

_____

CHAPTER
TWENTY - ONE

THE REMANT OF ISRAEL
GOD ALWAYS LEAVES A REMNANT

*"I ask then: Did God reject his people? By no means! I
am an Israelite myself, a descendant of Abraham, from
the tribe of Benjamin." (Romans 11:1 NIV).*

These are words of the Apostle Paul.

God did not reject the Hebrews, he punished them for
disobedience – primarily idolatry – in serving other
gods.

There is a difference! We are still here, a people
unto God, who is waiting on us to repent and return to Him.

*"The seed will grow well, the vine will yield its fruit, the
ground will produce its crops, and the heavens will drop
their dew. I will give all these things as an inheritance to
the remnant of this people. As you have been an object
of cursing among the nations O Judah and Israel, so will
I save you, and you will be a blessing. Do not be afraid,
but let your hands be strong" (Zechariah 8:12-13 NIV).*

REFLECTIONS

CHAPTER
TWENTY - TWO

WHAT'S YOUR REALITY?

Kathy Hughes, founder of *TV One* often used the tagline, *"What's Your Reality?"*

As I continue to unfold the truth of who African Americans are as a people, the tagline, "What's Your Reality?" rings out as loud as the Liberty Bell in Philadelphia. The same bell abolitionists used as a symbol to declare freedom from slavery. It is the same bell used in 1776 for the reading of the Declaration of Independence, notably known today as the 4th of July.

The reality of who African Americans are was birthed from a lie. There is no doubt so-called African Americans are searching relentlessly for their reality and identity in resources that do not exist, are hidden, and are lost forever.

We may find hope in learning new facts every February – our "allotted" time to discover new and wonderful things our ancestors contributed to society. Then twenty-eight days later, it gets pushed back for another year, and we get to make another small discovery. It is time out for that foolishness!

We can add the recent *"acknowledgment"* of **Juneteenth** to the list of *approved* celebrations. It wasn't until 2021 that many African Americans knew about Juneteenth, especially in the northern states. I only knew of Juneteenth because I lived in Texas for several years. It was never taught to me, and I had never heard of it. In my pure ignorance, I thought celebrating freedom two years after the fact was ridiculous. I did not understand the full impact back then. The reality is, *they* knew they were slaves while the rest were living under a false belief of freedom!

Juneteenth is only linked to freedom in America. We know who we are not, but we do not know who we are.

What are some visible characteristics of our current reality—walking around tattooed from head to toe, pants sagging, disrespect for elders in the community with foul/vulgar behavior? Even though we have the semblance of freedom, some of us walk in total bondage and darkness. Because the truth is, we will "never" be free until we come into the full truth and knowledge of who we are as a people special to God. So, we live out this "reality" others have forced upon us. We are better than that! We are of a royal priesthood!

What if we were to accept the reality that we are the original Hebrews of the Bible? Would it change your perspective, or should it change your perspective?

I believe we would have no choice but to straighten our backs and be encouraged to walk in dignity into our destiny. It would cause us to speak, dream, serve, and, most importantly, love differently, beginning with the love of self.

I was in a class once, and the instructor gave a statistic that the most educated person in either America or Detroit (not certain which was stated) is the African American woman. Not shocking, a southern white female from Tennessee spoke up and said she was "**shocked**." When queried by the instructor, she said, "well, you have all these 'single' mothers in Detroit." Now, what does that have to do with intelligence? But it is her "reality" and one bestowed upon black people. We are not the only ones who truly believe this lie, perpetuated since we were exiled from Africa. However, we certainly have accepted it as "reality."

We all have a point of reality. I challenge you, the reader, to check yours. Be honest with yourself and answer the question. What is my reality, and how am I living it out?

REFLECTIONS

_____

_____

_____

_____

_____

_____

_____

_____

_____

_____

_____

_____

_____

_____

_____

_____

_____

_____

_____

_____

_____

_____

REFLECTIONS

_____

_____

_____

_____

_____

_____

_____

_____

_____

_____

_____

_____

_____

_____

_____

_____

_____

_____

_____

_____

_____

_____

_____

_____

_____

_____

_____

CHAPTER
TWENTY - THREE

AFFIRMATIONS

T he following pages are designed to initiate critical thinking on what you have read. Each affirmation reflects what God says about you in His Word. As you read these affirmations, take them to heart. Journal what thoughts come to your mind upon reading them, whatever those thoughts may be. For example, the author of this book has lost her mind. The author of this book is on-point. The author of this book has given me a new direction toward a true light! Journal your thoughts.

Be open and honest with yourself. Challenge yourself and your belief system. Open your minds. What if this is true? What next?

Unchain your mind!

REFLECTIONS

God's Reality Check
The Beginning

There was a time in my youthful days I would begin reading a book starting with the last chapter first. Don't judge; I wanted to cut to the chase! That is where African Americans are. We have been trying to catch up on everything we missed by having the narrative of our beginning skipped. I was fortunate to have the book to go back to the beginning. However, our history books do not provide that to us. African Americans have been presented with a history that is missing the opening chapters of their existence in creation. We do not envision ourselves as part of God's narrative in Creation. But African Americans do have that history book. It is called the Bible.

Journey back with me to Chapter 1 of the Bible, to establish ourselves in the beginning.

> *"Then God said, let us make man in our image, after our likeness"* (Genesis 1:26; 28 ESV).

Meditate on that and answer the following questions:
Whose image was man-made in?

_____

_____

_____

Whose likeness was man-made in?

_____

_____

_____

What does that mean to you?

_____

_____

Affirmation: I was made in the image and likeness of God, and He blessed His creation. I was made in God's image regardless of what others say, think, believe, or feel. As a result, I am relevant, and my life does matter.

Prayer: Father God, thank you for creating me in your image and likeness. That assures me of my spiritual roots – even if I lack knowledge of my earthly branch, for it is the root that is grounded and anchored. Amen

Insight: Man was created from the dust of the earth in Africa. From the African Heritage Study Bible (Bible, 1993) we read; *"Even today's contemporary scholars verify that the first people of the earth were of African descent."*

_____

_____

_____

_____

_____

_____

_____

_____

_____

_____

_____

_____

_____

_____

_____

_____

_____

_____

God's Reality Check
The Fall of Man

When God created Man, he gave him free will, meaning man can make his own choices. Man is the only living creature that God gave that privilege to. The trees do not decide to sway with the wind. Animals do not have a choice in their navigation through life.

The first man and woman on earth, Adam and Eve, exercised free will. They chose to disobey God. As a result, all mankind born unto them now shares in the consequences of their actions. God did, however, provide a way of escape, with a choice to be reconciled back to Himself.

Scripture: Genesis 2:16-17:

"And the Lord God commanded the man, saying, you may surely eat of every tree of the Garden, but of the Tree of the Knowledge of Good and Evil, you shall not eat, for, in the day that you eat of it, you will surely die" (NIV).

Meditate: On the command: You may eat, except of …

_____

_____

_____

What key theme were Adam and Eve charged with?

_____

_____

_____

_____

_____

_____

_____

Obedience

They were given options. They chose to step outside the options given to them and made a bad choice. Read Genesis 3:1-24. In the narrative, we read that Eve was tempted by the serpent (Satan), ate of the forbidden fruit, gave some to Adam to eat, and their eyes were opened. In other words, they lost their innocence. God punished them for disobedience by removing them from the Garden of Eden. They had permission to eat of all, but…. They chose *the* but! There are consequences to the choices we make, whether good or bad.

Affirmation: I know God has a destiny for me, and I will be obedient to the path He sets before me.

Prayer: Father, your Word tells us that obedience is better than sacrifice. Help me to be obedient in all areas of my life. Amen

Insight: Obedience is non-negotiable. Disobedience is what got the Hebrews in trouble in the first place.

_____

_____

_____

_____

_____

_____

_____

_____

_____

_____

_____

The Punishment of the Hebrews

No one likes to be punished. In fact, we sometimes take the route of dishonesty and deny any wrongdoing to avoid punishment. As a parent, it is not always easy to punish our children. Yet some behaviors warrant it for course correction. The Hebrews were behaving contrary to their heritage in God's dwelling. They were warned of the consequences if they did not change. Instead, they chose to detach themselves from their Creator and behave like spoiled and privileged brats. Their actions resulted in God's hand punishing them.

Scripture: Zechariah 7:14:

"I scattered them with a whirlwind among all the nations, where they were strangers. The land was left so desolate behind them that no one could come or go. This is how they made the pleasant land desolate" (NIV).

Meditate: I scattered them.

Where were the Hebrews scattered and by whom?

_____

_____

_____

_____

_____

Affirmation: I may not be proud of what got us as a people to where we are, but at least I have the knowledge now to move forward in truth.

Prayer: Father, thank you for the whirlwinds of life that move us into a place of dependence on you. Amen.

The Call of God - Let My People Go
So, they Can Serve Me — God

God does not allow His people to remain in bondage. Carefully read the following scripture. Try to imagine yourself in this scene. Picture yourself enslaved, under the rule of someone who believes they have the right to keep you as their possession. What hope do you see for freedom?

Scripture: Jasher 79:35:

> *"And Pharoah said to Moses, what do you require? And they answered him saying, the Lord God of the Hebrews has sent us to thee, to say, send forth my people that they may serve me."*

Meditate: I was created to serve. God requires the oppressors of His people to set them free.

Affirmation: The Lord will deliver me out of the afflictions of this land, for His glory and His purpose!"

Prayer: Father, forgive me for drifting away from you, for serving idols of money, jobs, positions, and man. None of those things last, but serving you leads to a blessed and eternal life. I'm tired of trying it my way – strengthen me to follow yours. I will serve you because not only did you create me to serve you, but you have also delivered me time and time again; something no one else can do. Amen.

Insight: The Hebrews were in bondage due to consistent and constant disobedience. While they were in Egypt, they began to worship idols. God delivered them. While in America and scattered abroad, the Hebrews worshipped idols.

Their deliverance was to free them to come back to God. Who or what is your focal point of worship?

REFLECTIONS

The Promise of Restoration

God is a God of restoration. He restores the soul, the mind, the body, and the land – Anything in His creation can be restored. But He specifically speaks on the restoration of His chosen people in His Word.   You may recall the old nursery rhyme. Humpty Dumpty sat on a wall; Humpty Dumpty had a great fall. All the king's horses and all the king's men, couldn't put Humpty back together again? Humpty Dumpty was an egg head, sitting on a wall. He was fragile and in a vulnerable position, and when he fell his whole being cracked beyond repair.

God is the King of Kings and Lord of Lords. He can fix and restore what man cannot or what man has broken, even if broken and shattered. He can fix the soul and make it whole. His glue is grace, and it has a substance built into it called mercy. God is a restorer! When God restores, the result is better than the beginning.

Scripture: Jeremiah 30:1-4:

"This is the word that came to Jeremiah from the Lord: This is what the Lord, the God of Israel, says: Write in a book all the words I have spoken to you. The days are coming declares the Lord, when I will bring my people Israel and Judah back from captivity and restore them to the land, I gave their forefathers to possess says the Lord" (ESV).

Meditate: … God is Going to Restore His People!

Affirmation: I am not forgotten – God can restore whatever is broken in me.

Prayer: Father – we have been gone from our homeland so long that we do not even realize it is ours. Many of us have no desire to even visit. We have been aliens where we have been scattered – but await your timing of restoration. Keep us close to you – lest our hearts stray again." Amen.

REFLECTIONS

What Must I Do to be Reconciled Back to God?
The Redemption of Man

Reconciliation occurs when two or more individuals agree to come together and forgive each other's offenses. God has already done His part. It is up to mankind to do theirs'.

We have already been redeemed. When something is redeemed, it is bought with a price. For instance, when you take an item to a pawn shop to obtain a loan against that item, the pawn shop will hold it for a specified amount of time to allow you to retrieve or redeem it before it is sold. When you return for your item, and pay the redemption price, your loan is forgiven, and your item is returned to you. The debt is paid off. You purchase it back for a price. That is redemption. We were separated from God because of our transgressions.

Jesus paid the price for the sins of the world with his shed blood on Calvary. In other words, we were redeemed from our sins by the Blood of Jesus. Jesus' redeeming blood is an overflowing fountain of grace, mercy, love, forgiveness, and hope. He is waiting for us to return to Him while we still have time.

It is our turn to be reconciled to God. We do that through repentance, which is another way of saying turn away from behaviors counter to God's instructions.

Reconciliation takes communication. How do we communicate with God? Through prayer.

Man has already been redeemed. We need to be reconciled back to God while we still have time. Jesus is our Redeemer and Reconciler.

Scripture: Ephesians 1:7:

*"In him, we have redemption through his
blood, the forgiveness of sins, in accordance
with the riches of God's grace" (NIV).*

Meditate: My sins have been forgiven!

Affirmation: I have been redeemed.

Prayer: Father – thank you for redeeming me. Thank you
for the opportunity of reconciliation. Thank you for the ultimate
sacrifice of Jesus' shed blood to save my soul. Amen

REFLECTIONS

_____

_____

_____

_____

_____

_____

_____

_____

_____

_____

_____

_____

_____

_____

_____

_____

The Gift of Forgiveness

Forgiveness is an action that is often dismissed as an option due to a lack of understanding. It can also be dismissed or withheld due to feeling justified because of a wrong done to us. Forgiveness is especially challenging when that wrong cuts deep into the heart, body, or soul. In choosing not to forgive, we miss out on the blessings behind the action because we are operating in the way of the world and not the way of God. Forgiveness is a gift that does not require the other person's approval or acceptance. Jesus took on the penalty of death for our sins. Even on the cross after he was beaten mercilessly, Jesus forgave those responsible for his torture and ultimate death. Forgiveness takes the heaviness of carrying the wrong done to us away and frees us from the trap of becoming bitter. Bitterness is poison to the soul. When poison gets into our bodies, it is deadly.

The power and miracle of the act of forgiveness gives us the power to seek and extend forgiveness. It cannot be done in one's own strength. That is why it is so difficult to do. We erroneously believe that by not forgiving, we are pushing a little of that hurt back to the person who hurt us. Unfortunately, it does not work that way.

When we refuse to forgive, we refuse healing, deliverance, and freedom because there is a blessing in God's miraculous power behind the act of forgiveness. And it is to our benefit. Forgiveness was not withheld from mankind.

Scripture: 1 John 1:9:

> *"If we confess our sins, he is faithful and*
> *just to forgive us our sins and to cleanse*
> *us from all unrighteousness" (ESV).*

Meditate: Christ died and paid the ultimate sacrifice for me!

Affirmation: I am forgiven.

Prayer: Father – thank you for your gift of forgiveness. Help me to exercise the "give" in forgiving others. I cannot do it in my strength, but I can in yours. Thank you that your son did not withhold forgiveness from humanity that even after all they did to him, he cried out to forgive them. Amen.

REFLECTIONS

_____

_____

_____

_____

_____

_____

_____

_____

_____

_____

_____

_____

_____

_____

_____

_____

_____

_____

_____

REFLECTIONS

APPENDIX

Appendix A
Sample of Notable Blacks in the Bible and Society

Hebrew	Egyptian	Mixed	African
Abraham	Hagar	Ishmael	Ham
Mary	Simeon		Nimrod
Joseph	Pharaoh of Exodus (Possibly Ramses)		Cush
Jesus	King Tut		Canaanites
Joseph	Nefertiti		
Simon of Cyrene (Carried Jesus' Cross)	Queen of Sheba		
Paul			
Solomon			
Isaac (Jacob)			
David			
Moses			

Hebrew Tribes

Tribe	Location
Beta Israel Falasha	Ethiopia
Abayudaya	Uganda
Tutsi	Rwanda
Rusape	Zimbabwe
Lemba	South Africa
Ashanti, Ewe, Wefwi Wiawso	Ghana
B'nai Ephraim (Sons of Ephraim)	Yoruba, Nigeria
Lam-Lam	Timbuktu
Katsena, Ibo	Nigeria
Zafin Ibrahim	Malagasy Republic

Photos of woodcarvings in Kenya.
Photos by Jocelyn D. Whitehead

God gave Judah wisdom and knowledge to build and all manner of workmanship. Exodus 31:1

Photos by Jocelyn D. Whitehead

Photos by Jocelyn D. Whitehead

REFLECTIONS

About the Author
Min. Jocelyn Whitehead

Jocelyn Whitehead is a native of Detroit, a mother and grandmother. She is a photographer, speaker, teacher, and Minister of the Gospel, passionate about God's Word and people. Jocelyn has a bachelor's degree in Leadership and Ministry from Grace Christian University, where she graduated with high honors. She was honored by the Delta Epsilon Chi Association for Biblical Higher Education for Intellectual Achievement, Christian Character, and Leadership Ability.

Jocelyn has served on foreign and domestic mission trips. Her life's scripture is John 12:24, *"Truly, truly, I say to you, unless a grain of wheat falls into the earth and dies, it remains alone; but if it dies, it bears much fruit."*

Minister Whitehead is available
for speaking engagements and booksignings.
For more information, email
jocelyn@jocelynwhitehead.com

FOOT NOTES

CHAPTER 1

1 The Book of Jubilees is canonized in the Ethiopian Orthodox Church and by Ethiopian Jews, but it is not part of the Canonized versions of the Christian Bibles. It does provide rich historical context that compliments the texts in the Christian Bible. However, it is not a part of the canonized (authorized) 66 Books of the Christian Bible.

2 Dead Sea Scrolls are ancient manuscripts written on papyrus paper that were found in caves in 1948 in Qumran. Many of these scrolls were still in a condition that their authenticity could be confirmed. Along with these manuscripts – original manuscripts of canonized texts were also found, including texts from parts of Isaiah. See section on the Apocrypha for more information.

CHAPTER 2

1 *Demimonde - The class of women considered to be of doubtful morality and social standing (Merriam-Webster Dictionary).

A: a class of women on the fringes of respectable society supported by wealthy lovers; also: their world B: the world of prostitution.

B: a distinct circle or world that is often an isolated part of a larger world a night in the disco demimonde; especially: one having low reputation or prestige (Merriam-Webster Dictionary).

CHAPTER 3

1 Tudor Parfitt's original findings appear to have been watered down over the years. In his writings in 1999, he concluded that the Y Chromosome found in the Lemba people was rare, distinctly, and uniquely found in the Levites. Updated efforts have been made to resolve this as "oral tradition, and complicated scientific studies, to disprove the original findings."

2 Photo of Lemba Priests/Leaders (World Jewish Congress, 2010).

CHAPTER 5

1 400 Shekels = 10 pounds.

2 A cistern was a pit deep in the ground that stored water.

3 One Myriad = 10,000. Hence according to this account that would make it 120,000.

4 Tribe/Dispersion Column derived from (Facts & Details, 2018). However, there are various other views regarding this.

CHAPTER 6

1 Nephilim- Giants

2 Scripture references for the Book of Baruch are taken from The Revised English Bible with The Apocrypha (1995). Oxford University Press and Cambridge University Press.

CHAPTER 7

1 There are between 1500 and 2000 languages spoken in Africa!

2 No clarity is given on this comment, but it could explain where the stigma on Black men came from.

CHAPTER 8

1 Berean Standard Bible (2021). Online. https://biblegateway.com/versions

CHAPTER 15

1 https://blackhistory938.wordpress.com/2017/06/06/the-hebrew-israelites-and-the-trans-atlantic-slave-trade-connection/

CHAPTER 16

1 The US Government has initiated a bill that will celebrate or recognize the 400 years since so called Africans were brought to America, which is, in all actuality, confirmation to this scripture. (HR1242 – 400 Years of African American History Commission Act).

CHAPTER 19

1 Flogging involved beating a person with a whip that was made with small iron balls, or sharp pieces of sheep bones braided into leather straps. The whip would rip open the flesh – while the iron ball would bruise the body. The whip struck in a downward manner touching both sides of the back.

BIBLIOGRAPHY

Africa Resource. (n.d.). Retrieved from https://www.africaresource.com/rasta/sesostris-the-great-the-egyptian-hercules/the-list-of-african-tribes-who-are-descendants-of-the-hebrew-israelite-nation-by-nana-kofi/comment-page-1/

Bible, K. J. (1993). The Original African Heritage Study Bible. Nashville: The James C. Winston Publishing Company.

Douglas, J., & Tenney, M. (1987). Bible Dictionary. Grand Rapids, Michigan, United States of America: Zondervan.

Facts & Details. (2018, September). Retrieved from https://factsanddetails.com/world/cat55/sub389/entry-5710.html

Ginzberg, L. (n.d.). The Legends of the Jews Complete.

Hartford Courant. (1897, September 14). Negro Who Can Write Hebrew. Retrieved from Newspapers.com 2023.

Hubpages. https://hubpages.com/education/Seth-son-of-Adam-Found-in-West-Africa. (n.d.).

Josephus, F. (1987). The Works of Josephus - New Updated Edition. (A. William Whiston, Ed.) Peabody, MA: Hendrickson.

Johnson, K.T. (2013). Ancient Book of Jubilees. Bible Facts Ministries.

Lutz, L. (2002). When God Says Go. Grand Rapids: Discovery House Publishers.

Post, H. D. (2021, April 5). 1897: Educated African Jewish Man is Conceptually Confusing to Americans. Retrieved from https://aeprevost.wordpress.com/2016/10/26/1897-educated-african-jewish-man-is-conceptually/

Mayfield, C. (1965). People Get Ready, Lyrics Sony/ATV Music Publishing LLC, Chappell Music, Inc.

Merriam-Webster. (n.d.). Demimonde. In Merriam-Webster.com dictionary. Retrieved, 2023, from https://www.merriamwebster.com/dictionary/demimonde

Pratt, J. (2020, May 1). The Book of Jasher. Retrieved from https://www.johnpratt.com/items/docs/jasher.html Revised English Bible With Apocrypha. (1995). Oxford University Press, Cambridge University Press, Great Britain.

Revised English Bible With Apocrypha. (1995). Oxford University Press, Cambridge University Press, Great Britain

Rodgers, J. A. (1957). 100 Amazing Facts About the Negro with Complete Proof.

Tenney, M. (1987). Bible Dictionary. Grand Rapids, MI: Zondervan.

The Negroes in Negroland; The Negroes in America; and the Negroes Generally. (1808).

Thibedeaux, O. (2018). Pastor. New Orleans, Louisiana, United States of America.

Unknown. (2020, July 22). Retrieved from https://images.app.goo.gl/t75m48pez3TnJsEq7

Unknown, A. (n.d.). Retrieved from Web Document: https://www.google.com/search?q=drawing+garden+of+eden+map&safe=active&tbm=isch&tbo=u&source=univ&sa=X&ved=2ahUKEwiipfO-9bDdAhWkzIMKHSDSC-kQ7Al6BAgFEA0&biw=1246&bih=742#imgrc=Wy_xFNzTv4PIaM:

vomit. (n.d.) Random House Kernerman Webster's College Dictionary. (2010). Retrieved from https://www.thefreedictionary.com/vomit

Wade, N. (1999, May 9). DNA Backs a Tribe's Tradition Of Early Descent From the Jews. The New York Times. The New York Times.

Ward, C. D. (1998). The Equilateral Triangle. Retrieved 2018, from Logos Christian: https://www.logoschristian.org/triangle.html

World Jewish Congress. (2010, March 8). Lemba tribe in southern Africa has Jewish roots, genetic tests reveal. Retrieved 2018, from http://www.worldjewishcongress.org/en/news/lemba-tribe-in-southern-africa-has-jewish-roots-genetic-tests-reveal?printable=true